Science as Sacred Metaphor

Science as Sacred Metaphor

An Evolving Revelation

Elizabeth Michael Boyle, O.P.

LITURGICAL PRESS
Collegeville, Minnesota

www.litpress.org

Cover design by David Manahan, O.S.B.

Scripture quotations are taken from the New Revised Standard Version Bible, Catholic Edition, © 1989 by the Division of Christian Education of the National Council of Churches of Christ in the U.S.A., and are used by permission.

1   2   3   4   5   6   7   8

Library of Congress Cataloging-in-Publication Data

Boyle, Elizabeth Michael, 1927–
    Science as sacred metaphor : an evolving revelation / Elizabeth
Michael Boyle.
        p.   cm.
    Includes bibliographical references and indexes.
    ISBN-13: 978-0-8146-2404-3 (alk. paper)
    ISBN-10: 0-8146-2404-9 (alk. paper)
    1. Religion and science—Meditations.   2. Catholic Church—Prayer-
books and devotions—English.   I. Title.
BX1795.S35B69   2006
261.5'5—dc22

                                                          2006001614

Dedicated to

MARY OF NAZARETH

who

being neither scientist nor theologian

said "Yes" to the mystery

in whom all that exists

lives

and moves

and has its being.

CONTENTS

INTRODUCTION

You are not here to verify,
Instruct yourself, or inform curiosity.
. . . You are here to kneel
Where prayer has been valid.[1]

These words of T.S. Eliot, whose spiritual journey through science, metaphysics, and comparative religion concluded on his knees in his ancestors' chapel, announce the purpose of this book: to create a sacred space at the intersection where science and faith meet. For those who pray daily, the Word itself is the familiar meeting place, the door to one of those old, prayed-in churches, warm with the presence of all who have prayed there before us. The space to which I now invite the reader is like a new church, uninhabited by friendly ghosts, stripped of familiar icons and pious clutter, somewhat cold at first, but welcoming the light, waiting to be prayed into a home. In this place, scientific inquiry and the vision of faith will neither prove nor disprove each other. Instead, as its title suggests, both modes of perception will enrich each other through the poetic device of metaphor.

Scientists and theologians employ metaphor, not as literary ornament, but as a tool of discovery, analysis, and exposition. As such an instrument, sacred metaphor approaches scientific theories and discoveries as symbolic "texts" in an evolving revelation of divine truth. According to the evangelists, Jesus himself pointed to the physical world as a revelatory metaphor and a guide to the divine vision for life (e.g., Luke 12:22-27; John 12:24).Were he teaching today, the same Jesus who used the lives of birds and wildflowers as physical symbols for divine providence would probably be saying: "Consider the implications of lilies and stars, of quarks and quanta, earthquakes and volcanoes. Learn from the drama of life-out-of-death in everything from seeds to tsunamis."

When we are careful to avoid "reducing revelation to what can be humanly comprehended by analogy,"[2] metaphor can carry us to its own limits, where contemplative prayer takes over and becomes an act of communion with mysteries beyond comparison or paraphrase. Science, as well as the "secular" arts, can facilitate that participation. Historically, in the United States especially, the combination of science with religion has tended to provoke fears that erect walls covered with barbed wire. When science confirms our own most profound intuitions of the sacred, however, we can enter laboratories and observatories with the kind of reverence and awe once reserved for chapels and cathedrals. Through the concept of sacred metaphor, scientific exploration can open the door to prayer.

Obviously, a work based on such a subjective, poetic response to scientific material can be neither comprehensive nor systematic. Hence this volume is restricted to a highly selective sampling of those scientific theories that have confirmed and/or enhanced my personal faith experiences. Moreover, even as I use the term "sacred metaphor," I acknowledge that ever since the Incarnation destabilized all dualisms of sacred and profane, we can use the term "sacred" only to describe an *experience* of our own optimum humanity. John Haught, director of the Center for Science and Religion at Georgetown University, seems to endorse this form of validation when he writes about evolution as a mode of revelation:

> Religious thinkers can deal with evolution in a meaningful way only if they do so on the basis of their own experience of the sacred as mediated through the faith communities to which they belong.[3]

Distributed throughout these pages will be testimony from many whose careers in the natural sciences have strengthened their faith in the supernatural. Such creedal expressions by contemporary scientists, however, must not be invoked as "proof texts" for religious faith. As Sharon Begley warns in her introduction to *The Hand of God,* the impersonal mysterious force to which most scientists refer does not resemble the caring, intervening, personal God of the Judeo-Christian tradition.[4] At the outset, therefore, let me stipulate several basic premises concerning the nature of perception in science, poetry, and prayer.

Mystery & Metaphor: Some Basic Premises

❖ *First, all human knowledge is ultimately subjective.* Popular mythology to the contrary notwithstanding, purely "objective" science is an unscientific term. Still less legitimate are claims for a "purely objective" theology. All reputable scholars acknowledge the epistemological premise that *the knower conditions what is known*. Moreover, each knower, including the authors of Scripture and its interpreters, emerges from a historical intellectual context that includes constantly revised scientific data. In fact, historians of religion can demonstrate that since the beginnings of the human quest for knowledge, evolutions in theology have consistently followed revolutions in science.[5] No matter how neutral the language of the final presentation, the scholar's choices, the allure or disdain with which she engages her subject, all—for better and worse—pass through the sieve of individual personality and emerge as "embodied knowledge."[6] Scientists and theologians are no exceptions; poets never pretend to be. To paraphrase Emerson,[7] "There is no theology, only autobiography."

And just as human character develops in response to hardship, so throughout the history of ideas, progress seems to thrive on conflict. Over the past half century, in particular, some theologians seem to have benefited from the process once described by Arthur Koestler: "When two irreconcilable matrices of thought and experience coincide in the mind, the result is religious or scientific breakthrough."[8] Such breakthroughs have gradually modified, though far from dissolved, the legendary hostility between scientific and religious worldviews. During the last three decades, Christian scholars in increasing numbers have been publishing works that boldly endeavor not only to reconcile but arguably to enhance the Western religious tradition with contemporary scientific thinking. In the United States alone the last decades of the twentieth century witnessed the annual publication of over two hundred new titles interfacing science and religion.[9]

In my experience, theological pioneers exhibit two general temperaments. On the one hand, I have listened to the wild and witty spellbinder, a courageous maverick gleefully discharging six-shooters as he gallops over the Nicene Creed into a new frontier. His style seems dominated by a desire to shock, disturb, and take advantage of the current climate of eroded clerical credibility. On the other hand, I have read cautious, scholarly treatises whose exhaustive intellectual analyses conclude with the phrase "I have come to believe." For me, this sentence evokes the visual image of a head bowed in prayer, bathed in light from shattered stained-glass windows that open to the sky. Although writers of both types occasionally venture beyond where I am ready to go, I put my trust in a theology that appears to be forged in the crucible of prayer.

Study of these theologians has led me to the hypothesis that autobiography determines the limits of disbelief. For example, Dominican theologian Cletus Wessels, who has assiduously reexamined much traditional Catholic dogma in the light of evolutionary cosmology, reinterprets the doctrine of the Resurrection, not in terms of strict science, but in the light of what he has experienced personally since the death of his father.[10] Having reached my theory independently, I later came across cognitive research which concludes that people tend to seek data and interpret evidence to sustain beliefs. One such study concludes: "Both religious and anti-religious belief systems are often almost impervious to data."[11]

Some of us, who are neither scientists nor theologians, process both science and theology as poetry. The more I study spirituality in relation to science, the more I have become convinced that because of the inherent subjectivity of the human quest, personal faith experience (or the lack of it) predisposes some to reduce God to a mythic metaphor for science, while others celebrate science as a cosmic metaphor for God. For the former, eventually "nothing is sacred"; for the latter (including this author), everything is.

❖ Hence my second premise: *Both scientists and theologians make acts of faith as they explore parallel paths in the land of mystery.* Although many scientists insist that mystery is a temporary term for territory soon to be conquered by technology, that conviction itself constitutes a quasi-religious belief. For example, scientists engaged in the perennial search for a "Theory of Everything"[12] are motivated by their belief that there is one force, *the source beyond* and *the power within all that exists.* Admitting that they do not know *what it is,* scientists nevertheless attest *that it is.* With humiliating alacrity, skeptics dismiss each new development in the quest for the Theory of Everything with the type of scorn usually reserved for popular myth; for example, "This is the book archeologists may study for a rigorous, comprehensive view of how the twenty-first century inhabitants of the third rock from the sun believed the world worked."[13]

At the end of 2004, *The Edge,* a website devoted to science, published its annual question to scientists: "What do you believe is true even though you cannot prove it?"[14] Of the 120 respondents, only a handful named a religious dogma. Instead, secular scientists named over a hundred "scientific" concepts that they firmly believe are both absolutely true and absolutely unprovable. Two years before *The Edge* posed its provocative question, an international gathering of scientists celebrated the one-hundredth anniversary of quantum physics. Reporting the event, science writer Dennis Overbye commented that the field of quantum mechanics entertains "concepts that sound like mythology," for example, "that a sub-atomic particle like an electron can be in two places at once, everywhere or nowhere, until someone measures it."[15] In a scenario resembling the division of assets in a "friendly divorce," scientists and theologians seem to be ransacking each other's lexicons for a vocabulary to describe *mystery* that enjoys both secular sophistication and spiritual power.

❖ Therefore, my third and final preliminary premise: *The common language of science and religion is metaphor.* Both the content and the method of this book depend upon a nuanced grasp of this term. Neither metaphors nor symbols are "synonyms." Like the artist Magritte, writers must keep in mind that words themselves are like two-dimensional paintings—inadequate symbols of the reality they represent.[16] Paul Tillich goes so far as to say: ". . . a religious symbol is idolatrous unless it suggests its own inadequacy."[17]

Both adherents and opponents of the new science-based theologies must be wary of literalism, for in relation to God, all literalism is idolatry. For example, when scientific panentheists speak of the universe as "in God," they must be clear that nothing is "in" God as in a container, that all spatial locations of God are metaphors. Without observing this caveat, those scholars who exploit metaphor can sometimes replace biblical literalism with a physical literalism that is no more "true" than the illusion it is intended to supplant. The more attractive the metaphor, the more acute the danger of literalism, especially when either scientists or theologians invoke religion to invest their agendas with spiritual and ethical urgency. (One example of this physical literalism would be the abuse of ecofeminist Sallie McFague's widely quoted metaphor of the earth as "God's body.")[18]

Understood rightly, however, metaphor embraces something much richer and more exciting than equivalence. The finest definition of metaphor I have ever encountered was performed for me by Bernard Bragg, the actor known as the Lawrence Olivier of the National Theatre of the Deaf. Explaining that there is no "word" for metaphor in American Sign Language, he spontaneously invented a compelling visual poem. At first he held his hand before his face, mimicking a mirror; then he promptly rejected that static image. "A metaphor is more like the image in a swiftly moving stream," he continued signing, "a stream with shallows and depths, brightened by sun-darts, darkened by storm clouds overhead, freshened by melting snow and rainfall, widening and narrowing as it pursues its course." As each action generated new inspiration, the actor's performance itself became a metaphor for metaphor. Twenty-two years after this interview,[19] I came upon comments by the physicist-theologian Ian Barbour that read like a prosaic summary of Bragg's creative definition:

> A metaphor cannot be replaced by a set of literal statements because it is open-ended. . . . It cannot be paraphrased. . . .
>
> A metaphor is not an illustration of an idea already explicitly spelled out, but a suggestive invitation to the discovery of further similarities.
>
> The meaning of a metaphor survives at the intersection of the two perspectives that produced it.[20]

Following the brook of metaphor from the shallows of the known to the depths of the unknown can be a continual preparation for contemplation: "Dear Lord,/we lurch from metaphor to metaphor,/Which is—let it be so—a form of praying."[21]

Naming and Un-Naming God

As more and more scientists accept the premise that "science is a metaphorical enterprise at heart . . . , closer to philosophy and even theology than anyone thought fifty years ago," religious thinkers too must accept the limits of metaphor in relation to God, where it is truly "a strategy of desperation."[22] Hence, in this cross-disciplinary study we need to observe two related caveats. First, science enthusiasts often slip into a subtle inversion of the subject/predicate relationship in the science/theology equation. Even some contemporary theologians now seem to revert to ancient paganism's mode of making God a mythic version of science.[23] With deep respect for the revelations of science, this book reverses priorities, choosing science as one way of talking about God as the primary reality, with the universe and everything in it as the symbolic poem of God's self-revelation.

Second, and more importantly, awareness of metaphor, its power and its limitations, is nowhere more urgent than in thinking and speaking of God. As recently as 1988, John Paul II felt it necessary to remind us: "All language in relation to God—including the title Father—is by way of analogy, since God transcends all human experience, categories, and speech."[24]

Among contemporary scientists, and even theologians inspired by science, are those who scrupulously avoid "God language," some out of reverence for the Unpronounceable Name, some out of fear of losing respect in academia, most out of a profound and sincere agnosticism. As a result, scholars have generated a "New Age" thesaurus of neologisms for what lies beyond their senses. A sampling of such terms demonstrates how remarkably science has preempted the language of mysticism: "the parental void containing all ultimate secrets and underlying laws"; "the indefinable, immeasurable, unbroken whole that includes the entire universe"; "the ground for the existence of everything, including us." Atheistic synonyms for God run the gamut from huge—"the ocean of cosmic energy"—to subatomic: "the wave pulse which launched our universe." Oxymorons like Brian Swimme's "all nourishing abyss" and Dana Zohar's "quantum vacuum" replace references to a creator. Having reviewed all this tortuous nomenclature, Wessels opts for a metaphor to which one can pray: "unconditional, extravagant love."[25] Poets, for whom metaphor is *lingua franca,* are also the first to recognize its final inadequacy: "This God recedes from every metaphor,/this love shows/Itself in absence, which the stars adore."[26]

Thirteen Ways of Looking

Wallace Stevens' classic "Thirteen Ways of Looking at a Blackbird" can be read as a meditation on varieties of perception. Two stanzas in particular inspired the organization for this book:

Among twenty snowy mountains,
The only moving thing
Was the eye of the blackbird.

. . .

I do not know which to prefer,
The beauty of inflections
Or the beauty of innuendoes,
The blackbird whistling
Or just after.[27]

I have adopted Stevens' central metaphors to organize all chapters under uniform subtitles. Each chapter will begin with "Ways of Looking," that is, some preliminary definitions and distinctions for a general frame of reference. Next, in the section "The Eye of the Blackbird," I will elucidate how the scientific theory under discussion helps us to see God through *the moving eye of science.* Finally, under "Inflections and Innuendoes," I will suggest the implications of scientific theory for Christian faith in practice.

How to Use This Book in Preparation for Prayer

As a non-specialist, I can assure the reader with a limited knowledge of science that we do not have to be professional musicians to be moved by the beauty of music or to appropriate its wordless eloquence for prayer. Reflecting poetically and receptively on scientific data as a sacred text, we can go beyond analysis to enter into communion with the creative mystery at its heart. For several years my own pedestrian explorations in the world of science have developed into an informal ritual that those who read these pages might like to adapt to their own meditation on scientific materials. Every Tuesday morning as I peruse the pages of the *New York Times,* I turn to the science section to read reports of new discoveries ranging from astrophysics to microbiology. Then I reflect on these statements as one ponders the poetry of Scripture, praying to "see" the image of God and "hear" the hopes of God revealed through the evolving revelation of our sacramental universe.[28] Usually, out of this reflection comes a brief prayer. Finally, I let go of all data and images and rest in the Source of it all.

One could say that this little ritual, invisible to my companion at the other end of the breakfast table, has transformed the dining room into a "sacred place."[29] Sometimes the energy of that encounter carries me into further "participation" through reading and writing poetry. Those with limited time might prefer to use the brief quotations that open each chapter as texts for meditation. Individually or together, they could inspire a briefer ritual than the one I have described. Savoring the poetry and pondering the implications of these statements by scientists, mystics, and poets could open the door to contemplative prayer as verses of Scripture do.

Science headlines and poetry inspired by them act like a spacecraft's booster rockets. Once the mission is launched, the rockets must be discarded as unnecessary baggage. And sometimes truth will demand that we jettison other, more precious baggage—like our favorite ideas. Those who learn how to use science poetically to launch a fresh experience of faith will relinquish forever all hope of finding scientific "proof" for the book of Genesis or the content of the catechism. A broader understanding of revelation will empower them to emancipate themselves from all forms of idolatrous literalism, including some neo-pagan[30] worship of the "new science." Both challenged and reassured, they will continue their search through outer and inner space in the company of fellow explorers "Who are only undefeated/Because we have gone on trying."[31]

A Word About Language

Regrettably, many valuable citations from theologians and spiritual writers of earlier generations use masculine pronouns for the Deity. Copyright restrictions prevent my altering them. Moreover, retaining sexist language, far from enshrining sexist attitudes, can actually jar the reader into reexamining unacknowledged assumptions. As feminists themselves appreciate, every alteration of a text is a translation. "Translated works are Trojan horses, carriers of secret invasions. They open the imagination to new images and beliefs, new modes of thought, new sounds."[32] Already translation of Scripture into inclusive language has progressed from the invasion to the "occupation" stage, so that now citations in sexist language have the effect of drawing attention to outmoded imagery and beliefs. Our intention in the pages that follow is to spearhead simultaneously an invasion into and a retreat from a land whose poetry is finally untranslatable.

NOTES

[1] T. S. Eliot, "Little Gidding," in *The Complete Poems and Plays* (New York: Harcourt, Brace and Company, 1952).

[2] John Haught, *Mystery and Promise: A Theology of Revelation* (Collegeville, MN: Liturgical Press, 1993) 2.

[3] John Haught, *God after Darwin: A Theology of Evolution* (Boulder, CO: Westview Press, 2000) x.

[4] Sharon Begley, *The Hand of God: Thoughts and Images Reflecting the Spirit of the Universe,* ed. Michael Reagan (Philadelphia: Templeton Foundation Press, 1999) 27.

[5] See, for example, Edward Grant, *The Foundations of Modern Science in the Middle Ages* (Cambridge: Cambridge University Press, 1996); Gregory Riley, *The River of God: A New History of Christian Origins* (New York: HarperCollins, 2001).

[6] Sallie McFague, *Models of God: Theology for an Ecological, Nuclear Age* (Philadelphia: Fortress Press, 1987) 67. After 1962, Thomas Kuhn's widely read theory of the "paradigm-shift" influenced scientists to acknowledge that the criteria for judging scientific theories are "paradigm-dependent." *The Structure of Scientific Revolutions* (Chicago: Chicago University Press, 1970). Therefore, some surrendered the claim that science, as "theory-independent," is "objectively" superior to religion.

[7] "There is no history, only biography."

[8] Arthur Koestler, *The Act of Creation,* cited by Rosemary Haughton, *The Passionate God* (New York: Paulist Press, 1981) 1.

[9] For example, David C. Lindberg and Ronald L. Numbers, *God and Nature: Historical Essays on the Encounter Between Christianity and Science* (Berkeley: University of California Press, 1986); Fortress Press, "Theology and the Sciences Series"; Orbis, "Science and Religion Series"; as well as the publications of the John Templeton Foundation and the Center for Theology and Natural Science at Berkeley, California.

[10] Cletus Wessels, *Jesus in the New Universe Story* (Maryknoll, NY: Orbis Books, 2003) 124–125.

[11] Richard A. Nesbett and Lee D. Ross, *Human Inference: Strategies and Shortcomings of Social Judgment* (Englewood Cliffs, NJ: Prentice-Hall, 1980).

[12] "The ultimate explanation of the universe at its most microscopic level, a theory that does not rely on any deeper explanation . . . which would provide the firmest foundation on which to build an understanding of the world." Brian Greene, *The Elegant Universe: Superstrings, Hidden Dimensions, and the Quest for the Ultimate Theory* (New York: W. W. Norton, 1999) 17.

[13] George Johnson, "A Really Long History of Time," rev. Roger Penrose, *The Road to Reality: A Comprehensive Guide to the Laws of the Universe* (New York: Alfred A. Knopf, 2005); *New York Times Book Review* (2 February 2005) 14.

[14] *www.edge.org.* A sampling of responses was published under the title "God (or Not): Physics and, Of Course, Love: Scientists Take a Leap," *New York Times* (4 January 2005) F3.

[15] "Quantum Theory Tugged and All of Physics Unraveled," *New York Times* (12 December 2000) A2. The seven hundred physicists in attendance admitted *belief in,* but not *understanding of,* the theory considered to be the foundation of modern science.

[16] Magritte's most famous painting is a flat illustration of a smoker's pipe with a simple sentence superimposed: "Ce n'est-ce pas un pipe."

[17] Cited by Ian Barbour in *Myths, Models, and Paradigms: A Comparative Study in Science and Religion* (New York and San Francisco: Harper and Row, 1974) 14.

[18] Sallie McFague, *The Body of God: An Ecological Theology* (Philadelphia: Fortress Press, 1993). McFague first adopted the term introduced by process theologians Fisher and Hartshorne in her earlier *Models of God,* but it received wider currency after the publication of the eponymous volume.

[19] Personal Interview, Eugene O'Neill Theater Center, Waterford, Connecticut, 24 June 1982.

[20] Barbour, *Myths, Models, and Paradigms,* 14.

[21] Andrew Hutchins, "Praying Drunk," in *Upholding Mystery: An Anthology of Contemporary Christian Poetry,* ed. David Impastato (New York: Oxford University Press, 1997).

[22] McFague, *Body of God,* 33, 93.

[23] For example, Michael Morwood, *Praying a New Story* (Maryknoll, NY: Orbis Books, 2004); Diarmuid O'Murchu, *Evolutionary Faith: Rediscovering God in Our Great Story* (Maryknoll, NY: Orbis Books, 2003); *Quantum Theology: Spiritual Implications of the New Physics* (New York: Crossroad, 2003).

[24] John Paul II, "Mulieris Dignitatem: On the Dignity and Vocation of Women," *Origins,* vol. 18, no. 17, #8 (6 October 1988).

[25] Wessels, *Jesus in the New Universe Story,* 126ff., 136, et. al.

[26] Mark Jarman, "Sonnet 4," *Questions for Ecclesiastes* (Ashland, OR: Story Line Press, 1997).

[27] Wallace Stevens, *Wallace Stevens: Collected Poetry and Prose* (New York: The Library of America, 1996).

[28] The fact that I do not fully comprehend the scientific detail of all that I read does not diminish the sense of revelation in this process, for, with surprising frequency, my inspiration comes from a scientific "revelation" scientists admit they cannot fully comprehend either.

[29] ". . . sacred place is ordinary place, ritually made extraordinary." Belden C. Lane, *Landscapes of the Sacred: Geography and Narrative in American Spirituality* (Mahwah, NJ: Paulist Press, 1988) 19.

[30] The *New York Times* "Religion Journal," for example, reports that one of the fastest-growing religions in North America is "paganism, the umbrella term for all nature-based belief systems and spiritualities." It includes among its devotees many former Christians. Erin Goldscheider, "Witches, Druids, and Other Pagans Make Merry Again," *New York Times* (28 May 2005) B7.

[31] T. S. Eliot, "The Dry Salvages," in *The Complete Poems and Plays, 1909–1950* (New York: Harcourt Brace, 1980).

[32] Jane Hirshfield, "The World Is Large and Full of Noise: Thoughts on Translation," in *Nine Gates: Entering the Mind of Poetry* (New York: Harper Perennial, 1997) 56.

Chapter One

REFLECTIONS ON
A QUANTUM UNIVERSE

"For your immortal spirit is in all things."
(Wisdom 12:1)

"Nature is visible spirit, and spirit is invisible nature."
(Friedrich Schelling)[1]

"Everyone who is seriously involved in the pursuit of science
becomes convinced that a spirit is manifest in the laws of the Universe
—a spirit vastly superior to that of man. . . .
In this way the pursuit of science leads to a religious feeling of a special
sort . . . quite different from the religiosity of someone more naïve."
(Albert Einstein)[2]

"Thinking of God as the living awareness in the space between the atoms
. . . gets us past some of the great theological divides. . . .
Is God immanent or transcendent, internal or external, composed or
compassionate?
Like the question of whether the atom is a wave or a particle,
The answer is 'Yes.'"
(Tom Mahon)[3]

"Your kingdom come
To this out-of-the-way corner of the universe
With its 90% of matter that is invisible."
(Ernesto Cardenal)[4]

Those who view the world through the twin oculars of faith and science find the language of the laboratory and the planetarium a rich source of metaphors for imagining realities inaccessible to the senses. Each day, advances in technology expand the boundaries of visible creation by exposing worlds-within-worlds heretofore invisible to the naked eye. Meanwhile, throughout the final decades of the twentieth century, with increasing insistence, some theologians have also expanded the traditional parameters of the biblical phrase "according to God's likeness" to embrace not only Jesus Christ and humanity but also all creation.[5] As quantum physics penetrates ever deeper into the interior of nature's subatomic wilderness, worshiping Christians reflect: "How does this universe also mirror the divine image?" In this spirit some speculations of theology and of quantum physics can be read as parallel epiphanies. When we approach the discoveries of science prayerfully, with reverence like that which we bring to the written Scriptures, these parallel texts can put us in touch with our own sacredness, *even and especially when we do not fully understand their technical detail.*

For centuries ordinary human beings have most often recorded their sense of the sacred in the presence of *immensity*. Oceans, mountains, canyons, outer space—all stun us into inner silence and provoke a nameless gratitude for our participation in something incomprehensibly vast. The revelations of quantum physics invite us to experience this same awe in the presence of the *infinitesimal*. Quantum theory suggests that the mystics' intimations of an energy "whirling," "circling, encompassing," "quickening," and "permeating"[6] every visible reality have a basis in the "hard sciences," that there is, in fact, "something more" within and beyond our most compelling sense experiences.

Ways of Looking: Definitions and Distinctions

How exactly do we define a *quantum universe?* It is both a relief and a dilemma to learn that very few professional scientists claim competence to explain quantum theory clearly to non-scientists. Yet, to an adult who has devoted a lifetime to the two professions of religion and literature, the world exposed by quantum physics is not unfamiliar, and I find myself in the position of Moliere's "Bourgeois Gentilhomme," who was astonished to discover that he had been "speaking prose all his life."

Quantum theory offers a scientific synonym for that invisible hemisphere of reality that many of us have known personally and/or read about in poetry and mystical literature all our lives. While the mystics and poets have long compelled respect for their ecstatic intuitions of quantum theory, I have come to believe that contemporary science forces us to do more than that. Science forces us to *own* its spiritual implications and moral imperatives. So, for the spiritually committed but scientifically uninitiated, here is a brief introduction to some "bare bones" of quantum theory that can enhance our idea of God.

In the context of spirituality, perhaps it is best to define the quantum universe not as a world but as a worldview, the scientific worldview that began to open up in the 1920s, when scientists replaced the classical universe of *solid objects* with an invisible network of *energy* in particles, fields, waves, and flows. Incredibly powerful microscopes have revealed that nothing that we see is a "thing" at all. Every speck of physical matter is, in fact, a minute, even subatomic *event* within a vast web of activity. It was Einstein who first named the microscopic "bundles of energy" discovered by Max Planck "quanta," and throughout the ensuing century new discoveries have spawned a whole new lexicon of terms to distinguish smaller and smaller, more and more dynamic subquantum phenomena. Since the splitting of the atom over sixty years ago, the smallest particle, graphically depicted as a tiny solar system with numberless electrons orbiting around its central nucleus, has undergone continual revision wherein each particle resembles an infinitesimal, hyperactive "system" whose protons and neutrons have been analyzed to distinguish at least twelve kinds of *quarks*. These in turn demanded new vocabulary to identify *neutrinos, muon-neutrinos, tau-neutrinos,* and eventually *anti-particles.*[7]

Moreover, experiments by quantum physicists have revealed that the behavior of everything perceptible to the senses is governed, not by immutable laws, but by constantly shifting relationships and interactions within and among all the occupants of the cosmos. Quantum physics stipulates a series of contrasts with classical physics (which prevailed from the seventeenth through the twentieth centuries).

- In contrast to the classical notion of a "higher cause" producing dependent "effects," quantum theory postulates a web of mutually interdependent *interactions.*
- In contrast to the ultimately discoverable and reliable *laws* that classical physics promises, quantum physics offers *probability* in interactions and relationships at every level. By way of compensation for this risky *unreliability,* quantum physics offers the more attractive risk of *co-creativity.*

- In contrast to the classical image of a clockwork universe in which the whole is the sum of its discrete parts, quantum theory postulates a unifying gestalt: neither the whole universe nor anything in it can ever be reduced to its components any more than a human person can be reduced to body parts.
- In contrast to the strict hierarchy of being in the classical cosmos, a mutual interdependence of being blurs the distinction between "living" and non-living.

In summary, quantum theory advocates what Diarmuid O'Murchu calls "a quality of mystical receptivity" to the evolving nature of life at all levels, replacing the human struggle for dominance with "respect for life's inherent processes."[8]

Nothing in the above synopsis sounds really new, for the vision of quantum physics has gradually permeated the Western cultural mainstream in everything from ecology to religion to politics to literary theory. In a rudimentary way, most of us have been "speaking quantum" all our lives without knowing it. Hence one need not be a physicist nor understand the details of quantum theory to recognize its implications for contemporary Christian spirituality.

The Eye of the Blackbird: How Quantum Theory Helps Us to "See" God

Science, like theology, offers a way to "see" God through metaphor. Quantum science offers a vivid image for the traditional church teaching that "God is everywhere," as well as for our deepest personal intimations of a divine energy within and around us. A universe that is in motion in every atom of its being seems like a dazzling mirror for the God Aquinas defined as "Pure Act." An invisible world moving so rapidly that it seems to stand still seems an apt metaphor for the philosopher's "unmoved Mover," to which T. S. Eliot added warmth and intimacy: "Love is itself unmoving/Only the cause and end of movement."[9]

Quantum science also reminds us, however, that the God humanity once created in the image of classical physics, that is, a clockmaker who can be blamed for all defective parts and expected to repair every malfunction, can no longer be invoked by thoughtful Christians. Quantum science replaces this distorted image of God with one that becomes radically respectful of God's freedom and our own.

Of course, science itself does not define the energy within and around the universe as divine, nor should we carelessly conflate scientific and theological terminology or unconsciously equate creation with the creator. Wessels, among theologians whose language about God is under continual revision in the light of modern science, nevertheless offers several important distinctions for us to keep in mind:

> God and nature are not identical, but they are also not separable.
> . . . In an emerging universe . . . every being and every activity flows from the inner presence of God, and there is no way to separate the natural from the supernatural.[10]
>
> . . .
>
> Our loving God is clearly *other than* and infinitely *more than* the universe, but God is also inseparable from every being in the universe . . . God is both immanent and transcendent simultaneously."[11]

Here Wessels seems to agree with Aquinas, who subsumes immanence within transcendence: "Things are more in God than God is in things."[12]

For Christians in particular, therefore, God is not a dualist: *everything is innately spiritual.* In the past this intuition of the mystics made them objects of suspicion for theological watchdogs on the alert for symptoms of pantheism. Now many theologians applaud the mystics for having anticipated our modern contempt for dualism, while physicists invent terms like "implicate and explicate order" to explain their claim that an entity or an event can be simultaneously "immanent" and "transcendent."[13]

In our culture, intimations of an ambient spirituality are often brutally overwhelmed by the apparent triumph of materialism. For the most part, the task of articulating the *interiority* of matter that science affirms has been performed by poets. Jesuit poet Gerard Manley Hopkins died thirty years before Planck and Einstein published, yet poetic experience immersed him intuitively in the energetic inner life of nature that these scientific geniuses later described in physical terms. To Hopkins, whose world was "charged with the grandeur of God,"[14] every entity in nature was a revelatory and sacramental event, a glimpse into a hyperkinetic, inexhaustibly various mirror of the creator. Not only in human souls but also in the inner life of inert stones as well as soaring falcons, Hopkins recognized and celebrated *individuality* as a myriad expression of the divine face. For the distinctive interior landscape of each physical phenomenon Hopkins coined the word "inscape." Again and again, he struggled to translate into unique synaesthetic imagery the *instress* through which this inscape communicates itself. The opening octet of one of his famous sonnets fairly vibrates with quantum energy:

> As kingfishers catch fire, dragonflies draw flame;
>   As tumbled over rim in roundy wells
>   Stones ring; like each tucked string tells, each hung bell's
> Bow swung finds tongue to fling out broad its name;
> Each mortal thing does one thing and the same
>   Deals out that being indoors each one dwells;
>   Selves—goes itself; myself it speaks and spells,
> Crying *What I do is me: for that I came.*[15]

In the concluding sextet Hopkins seems to spell out in the spiritual order what quantum physicists concluded after a long and strenuous debate about the behavior of the tiniest material phenomena, namely, that they are both particles and waves *simultaneously*. The ideal Christian, declares the poet, is in the same instant *autonomous* and *connected*. At the height of ecstatic autonomy, the poet finds himself at the center of the most profound *communion* and calls himself to responsible action:

> I say more: the just man justices;
>   Keeps grace that keeps all his goings graces;
> Acts in God's eyes what in God's eyes he is—
>   Christ. For Christ plays in ten thousand places,
> Lovely in limbs, and lovely in eyes not his
>   To the Father through the features of men's faces.

Hopkins' apprehension of the quantum universe that science had yet to discover forced him to invent unconventional prosody and syntax to convey a dynamism for which English grammar and metrics were too tame. Nevertheless, his spirituality is orthodox, and the demands of his eccentric style are less challenging than his clear theme: whenever we are profoundly present to the natural world, God is profoundly accessible to us. Together we operate from the center of an invisible energy that draws us simultaneously inward and outward, making us both autonomous and connected, both free and responsible, centered deep within ourselves and a part of something bigger than ourselves, accountable to and for brothers and sisters—human and other-than-human—whom we shall never meet.

The paradox of autonomy and interdependence is further refined in the quantum physics of *holon theory*. Introduced by Arthur Koestler a quarter century ago,[16] holon theory postulates that whatever exists—in biology, cosmology, psychology, theology—represents both a whole and a part. Every whole forms a part of something bigger while not ceasing to be whole in itself. Once again, science is confirming a vision of reality that poets and mystics expressed long ago. William Blake's version is often quoted:

> To see a World in a grain of Sand
> And a Heaven in a Wild Flower,
> Hold Infinity in the palm of your hand
> And Eternity in an hour.[17]

Blake anticipates the quantum universe Brian Greene describes over a century later: "At the moment of the big bang, the whole of the universe erupted from a microscopic nugget whose size makes a grain of sand look colossal."[18] This holon experience, intuited psychologically as "the self meeting the Self," can be found in the literature of every religious tradition.[19]

When I read holon theory the first time, a shock of recognition brought back my most cherished memory, an incident I believe I can now call a holon experience. My older brother and I were out looking for wildflowers to place on our May altar at home. We crossed our favorite brook into a field of tall, sun-drenched weeds. Eventually we separated, and as dusk approached, I began to feel chilly. The weeds still retained some warmth, so I lay down in them and looked up into the sky. All at once the silence reached down and held me. God seemed to be simultaneously above, below, and within me, at once infinitely distant and intimately close, immense, yet focused to a pinpoint that was both myself and something more than myself. I have no idea how long this moment lasted, for time ceased until I felt my brother shaking me and calling my name.

The next day I hurried back to the field alone. I lay down in the weeds and waited, but nothing happened. I stood up and called out to the sky, "Hello God!" but no one answered. Then I noticed a little hillock of violets nearby. Instinctively, I knelt and buried my face in them and whispered, "Hello God." Then, for the first time in my life, I thought I knew where God wanted to be found: I hugged myself and murmured over and over into my own chest, "Hello God, Hello God!" The moment ended abruptly as I tasted the salt of strange tears. The God I addressed in that encounter had neither face nor form nor gender. The Presence bore no resemblance to anything in my imagination or vocabulary. I was nine years old.

Paul Tillich tells us: "One can never grasp the object of faith, but one can be grasped by it."[20] In that childhood incident I was "held" by something I could never grasp, and that moment was and continues to be the quintessence of an "intimacy" for which all other uses of the word are inadequate metaphors. I believe almost everyone has episodes like this in which we are possessed and dispossessed by something we cannot define, deserve, or deny. Scientist David Bohm hints at this mystery in his attempt to define the holon experience: "a wholeness which is both immanent and transcendent, and which, in a religious context, is often given the name of God. The immanence means that what *is* is immanent in matter; the transcendence means that this wholeness is also beyond matter."[21] Reflecting on holon theory can in itself open us to a momentary apprehension of the transcendent/immanent phenomenon Bohm describes.

Poetry concurs with science that "the numinous does not discriminate, . . . infinitude and oneness do not exclude anyone."[22] The mystical poetry of Francis Thompson, for example, demonstrates that an intimate experience of God's presence through creation is not reserved for "nice" people. An academic failure, an addict, and frequently a homeless person, the poet, not surprisingly, found a kindred spirit in the Book of Job, which Terrence Connolly suggests might be an unconscious inspiration for some lines:

> But ask the animals, and they will teach you;
> the birds of the air, and they will tell you;
> ask the plants of the earth, and they will teach you;
> and the fish of the sea will declare to you" (Job 12:7-8).[23]

At once acknowledging and demolishing the traditional "hierarchy of being," Thompson exhorts us to enter into communion with God through contemplation, not only of the stars but also of the souls of derelicts and of our own clay-shuttered psyches.

The Kingdom of God

O world invisible, we view thee,
O world intangible, we touch thee,
O world unknowable, we know thee
Inapprehensible, we clutch thee!

Does the fish soar to find the ocean,
The eagle plunge to find the air—
That we ask of the stars in motion
If they have rumor of thee there?

Not where the wheeling systems darken,
And our benumbed conceiving soars!—
The drift of pinions, would we hearken
Beats at our own clay-shuttered doors.

The angels keep their ancient places;—
Turn but a stone, and start a wing!
'Tis ye, 'tis your estrangèd faces,
That miss the many-splendoured thing.

But (when so sad thou canst not sadder)
Cry;—and upon thy so sad loss
Shall shine the traffic of Jacob's ladder
Pitched twixt heaven and Charing Cross.

Yea, in the night, my Soul, my daughter,
Cry,—clinging Heaven by the hems;
And lo, Christ walking on the water
Not of Gennesareth, but Thames!

Francis Thompson[24]

Among those for whom mystical experience reaches into silence, it is not surprising to find poets who "speak in the light of having experienced that which is now missing."[25] Marion Goldstein's reflection on holon theory unconsciously continues that tradition.

Holon

The Physicist can not prove
Every whole is
Simultaneously
A part
And every part
Is Simultaneously
A whole
In the ever-emerging
Connectedness
Of the universe
There is always the absence
Even when full
A field
Spilling yellow daffodils
Beckons
Lie in my golden arms
A moment
Whole
But no, what's missing
Is the absence
Of more
Always this yearning
For what is hidden
Like the black bird
Deep in a bush
You can not see
Until it flies away
You know
Like God.

Marion Goldstein[26]

Inflections and Innuendoes
How Quantum Physics Calls Us to Serve God

Reflecting on the scientific theories outlined in this chapter should, first of all, energize us with encouragement that our smallest endeavors have global "relevance." According to quantum physics, there is no such thing as a solitary inhabitant or an isolated activity in the universe. Just

as particles are also simultaneously waves reachin
and interacting across great distances, so
self-transcendence that comes about b
tion and communion. As in human
engenders a new reality. At every le
to fulfillment through transformatic
language in John's Gospel: "Unless i
and dies, it remains just a single grain; .
(John 12:24).

In many ways quantum reality mirrors the way the life of a contemplative individual affects the whole world. His or her level of consciousness and level of charity are nodes of spiritual energy simultaneously
autonomous and invisibly yet powerfully *connected* to the whole body of
the world by way of self-transcendence. Meditating on holon movement
can also call us to the interactive dimension of Eucharist. Holon theory
makes us see that the sacrament of Holy Communion, once considered
an intensely private act, reaches fulfillment in the commitment to *give* as
well as *receive* Holy Communion. For centuries Christians have known
the invisible drama of giving and receiving spiritual energy as the Communion of Saints.[27] Quantum physics extends the concept by calling us
to a global holonomy as a form of ecumenical worship. Worship, ideally,
calls the worshiper to resist competitive consumerism, for holonomy
with the planet and the universe sings a hymnody more pleasing to God
than an anthropocentric chorus of soloists.

Like the written Scriptures, scientific data yield life-altering insights
only after long and prayerful attention in the light of holistic experience.
When one meditates faithfully on these parallel texts, when one opens a
scientific text or news item with the prayer "Speak Lord, your servant is
listening" (1 Sam 3:10), by degrees one begins to recognize "the divine
in what is not divine"[28] and to replace dead metaphors with live ones.
Gradually the quantum universe emits energetic hints at the mysterious
life of the Trinity, in what one ecotheologian describes as "a mystery
of engaged living, a loving, personal communion that erupts eternally
within God's own being and explodes into a fragmented universe (at
least one), fraught with the force of God's own exuberance."[29] Such
imagery will prove more soul-satisfying than pictures of an old man,
a young man, and a bird. At the practical level, we can hope that this
exchange of metaphors will cleanse our faith and deepen its level of
engagement. Meditating on quantum physics should propel us, once

and for all, out of the devout and self-deceptive posture that waits in a broken world calling on omnipotence to "come down" and "fix it."

Since poets' intuitions frequently predate the discoveries of science, a "new discovery" often resembles poetry written long ago. For example, the following poem juxtaposes a news article published in 2004 with lines written before the "new" scientists were born.

Supersolid

T. S. Eliot, you old plagiarist!
Outdone yourself at last—
stolen the words
right out of the mouth
of the future.

> *At the still point of the turning world,*
> *Neither flesh nor fleshless,*
> *a white light, still and moving.*
> *At the still point there is only the dance.*[30]

Three quarters of a century later
quantum midwives cry:

> *The whole system is undergoing*
> *a coordinated movement like a ballet dance.*
> *Helium spinning at white heat*
> *gives birth to a freezing supersolid.*

> *Neither gas nor fluid*
> *a new state of being!*
> *"It's going to make us rethink*
> *our whole concept of 'solid.'"*[31]

But you were there first, old friend,
burning in the dry ice of faith
freezing one half degree above
absolute zero
spinning toward the still point
where your partner disappears
into the dance, the only solid
solid in our fragile universe.

Elizabeth Michael Boyle, O.P.

NOTES

[1] Freidrich Schelling, "Ideas for a Philosophy of Nature," cited in Lynn Gamwell, *Exploring the Invisible: Art, Science, and the Spiritual* (Princeton: Princeton University Press, 2000) 13.

[2] Letter to a child who asked if scientists pray (24 January 1936), Einstein Archive 42-601.

[3] Tom Mahon, "The Spirit in Technology," cited in Michael Reagan, ed., *The Hand of God: Thoughts and Images Reflecting the Spirit of the Universe* (Philadelphia: Templeton Foundation Press, 1999) 139.

[4] Ernesto Cardenal, *Cosmic Canticle,* trans. John Lyon (Williamantic, CT: Curbstone Press, 1993).

[5] For example, Mary Catherine Hilkert, O.P., *Imago Dei: Does the Symbol Have a Future?* Santa Clara Lectures, vol. 8, no. 3 (Santa Clara University, 14 April 2002); Denis Edwards, "For Your Immortal Spirit Is in All Things: The Role of the Spirit in Creation," in *Earth Revealing—Earth Healing: Ecology and Christian Theology,* ed. Denis Edwards (Collegeville, MN: Liturgical Press, 2001) 45–61.

[6] Hildegard of Bingen, "Antiphon for Divine Wisdom," in *Symphonia: A Critical Edition of the Symphonie Aemonie Celestium Revelationum,* trans. Barbara Newman (Ithaca: Cornell University Press, 1988).

[7] Brian Greene, *The Elegant Universe: Superstrings, Hidden Dimensions, and the Quest for the Ultimate Theory* (New York: W. W. Norton and Company, 1999) 7.

[8] Diarmuid O'Murchu, "What Is the Quantum All About?" in *Quantum Theology: Spiritual Implications of the New Physics* (New York: Crossroad, 2003) 23–35.

[9] T. S. Eliot, "Burnt Norton," in *The Complete Poems and Plays* (New York: Harcourt, Brace and Company, 1952).

[10] Cletus Wessels, *Jesus in the New Universe Story* (Maryknoll, NY: Orbis Books, 2003) 33.

[11] Ibid., 58.

[12] Joseph Pieper, *The Human Wisdom of Saint Thomas: A Breviary of Philosophy from the Works of Saint Thomas Aquinas,* trans. Drostan MacLaren (New York: Sheed and Ward, 1948) 87.

[13] David Bohm, *Wholeness and Implicate Order* (New York: Routledge and Kegan Paul, 1980).

[14] "God's Grandeur," in *Hopkins: Poems and Prose,* Everyman's Library Pocket Poets (New York: Alfred A. Knopf, 1995).

[15] Ibid. "As Kingfishers Catch Fire."

[16] Arthur Koestler, *Janus* (London: Hutchinson, 1978).

[17] William Blake, "Auguries of Innocence," *The William Blake Archive,* ed. Morris Eaves, Robert N. Essick, and Joseph Viscomi (4 November 2005): http://www.blakearchive.org.

[18] Greene, *Elegant Universe,* 4.

[19] Jane Hirshfield, *Women in Praise of the Sacred: 43 Centuries of Spiritual Poetry by Women* (New York: HarperCollins, 1994) xix.

[20] Paul Tillich, *Shaking the Foundations* (New York: Charles Scribner's Sons, 1996) 27.

[21] "A Conversation with David Bohm," *The Holographic Paradigm and Other Paradoxes,* ed. Ken Wilber (New York: The New Science Library, 1982) 187–188.

[22] Hirshfield, *Women in Praise of the Sacred,* xix.

[23] *Poems of Francis Thompson,* ed. Rev. Terrence L. Connolly, S.J. (New York: D. Appleton Century, 1941) 555, nn. 5–6.

[24] Published in 1908 under the title "In No Strange Land," with the subtitle "The kingdom of God is within you," 554, n. 1.

[25] Hirshfield, *Women in Praise of the Sacred,* xx.

[26] Marion Goldstein's use of scientific metaphor for spiritual realities inspired her award-winning chapbook *Psalms for the Cosmos* (Johnstown, OH: Pudding House Publications, 2003).

[27] Wessels, *Jesus in the New Universe Story,* 51.

[28] Edwards, "For Your Immortal Spirit Is in All Things," 61.

[29] Anthony Loewes, "Up Close and Personal: In the End, Matter Matters," in *Earth Revealing—Earth Healing,* 133.

[30] Fragments from "Burnt Norton," in *The Complete Poems and Plays* (New York: Harcourt, Brace and Company, 1952).

[31] "Only in Quantum Physics: Spinning While Standing Still," *New York Times* (21 September 2004) F3.

Chapter Two

REFLECTIONS ON DYNAMIC LANDSCAPES

"I heard . . . you in the garden, and I was afraid."
(Genesis 3:10)

"The voice of the Lord shakes the wilderness. . . . and strips the forest bare."
(Psalm 29:8-9)

"If we accept the premise that creation is God's voice, and if we listen to that voice as a matter of conscience, we must acknowledge that from its polluted streams, radioactive soil, and deforested landscapes, the voice of God is crying out in pain."
(Elizabeth Johnson)[1]

"The antiquity of a tree is a concentration of cosmic energy."
(Stanley Kunitz)[2]

"And now abideth faith, hope, gravity, These three, but the greatest of these Is the ground."
(Frederick Seidel)[3]

"Civilization exists by geologic consent."
(Will Durant)[4]

Landscape is every child's first science teacher. It is also every thoughtful adult's perennial spiritual director. In two contrasting Gospel texts in particular, the evangelists show Jesus highlighting the wisdom of the earth itself, advising his followers to look for spiritual guidance in God's revelations expressed through the beauty and death surrounding them: "Consider the lilies, how they grow" (Luke 12:27; Matt 6:27-30), and "Unless a grain of wheat falls into the earth and dies . . ." (John 12:24). In miniature, these two Scriptures prefigure the wise counsel still available from the inspiring—and sometimes threatening—landscapes of our lives. Reflecting on landscapes, even the deracinated remnants that have survived human exploitation, introduces us to a personal relationship with science that can enhance our interpretation of Scripture.

Ways of Looking: Definitions and Distinctions

Before turning to the lilies themselves, it is interesting to meditate on some definitions of the verb "consider." The original Greek of the Gospel *(kata-noeō)*, "fixing the eye of the spirit on," is language appropriate to the evangelist's first audience. For English readers, several linguistic generations removed from the original, the verb takes on new meaning. Derived from the Latin *con-sidere*, "to place alongside the stars,"[5] the verb suggests a way of looking at everything on earth, including ourselves, in relation to astrophysics. An ecotheologian's meditation on providence accords a field of wildflowers the same respect as distant galaxies.

Such reflection involves reordering our concept of providence to regard landscapes and all the living beings that populate them in the context of cosmic interdependence. Since the time the New Testament was written, optical technology has greatly enhanced our capacity—and our responsibility—to "consider" all things in relation to the stars and to place ourselves in the company of all the still-evolving, co-dependent children of the stars. By extension, a scientific interpretation of this text instructs us to cultivate a cosmological perspective on all pedestrian events. In this enterprise the eye of faith and the eye of science can enhance each other, for scientific technology sees more than the naked eye, while the soul's lens penetrates to even wider and deeper meaning than that of the telescope or microscope.

Although scientists, poets, and contemplatives engage in a common search for ultimate truth, two vital differences distinguish scientists from their companions in this quest. First, the scientist goes into fields and forests and interplanetary space to *find the truth;* the poet/contemplative goes there *to be found.* Very often, the landscape *where the holy initiates this intimate encounter* becomes defined as a sacred place.[6] Second, although scientific method begins with an act of imagination, it relies for verification on *observation,* whereas poetic intuition and natural mysticism move from imagination and physical observation to knowledge by *participation.* The prayer of the eyes is to look at each thing until it looks back. Spiritual communion with natural phenomena becomes for the contemplative *a way of knowing and being known.* In his famous essay "Nature," Ralph Waldo Emerson records this kind of experience, one that echoes throughout nature poetry and mystical literature in all ages and tongues:

> Standing on the bare ground—my head bathed in the blithe air and uplifted into infinite space,—all means of egotism vanish. . . .
> I am nothing. I see all.
> The currents of the Universal Being circulate through me; I am part and parcel of God.[7]

While poets, artists, and mystics give the clearest expression to such communion with landscape, the process is far from esoteric. In our most familiar encounters with natural beauty, even and especially in childhood, well-loved forests, mountains, seascapes, and even urban neighborhoods take root in our emotional "inscapes" and grow into the imagery of ourselves and of God. Like parents, these images both nourish and admonish, leaving patterns of affective behavior encoded in the unconscious for a lifetime. From the psalms, to the Romantic poets, to the American Transcendentalists, poets have personified their encounters with landscape first as Presence and then as moral guide. Hence, when a landscape is sacrificed on the altar of commerce, our first and often deepest wound is the loss of an irreplaceable trysting place where immanence meets transcendence. To extend to the sciences the personal relationship we enjoy with our most-cherished landscapes requires an act of the imagination. But, beyond that, cultivating friendship with the sciences as they reveal to us the interior lives of our natural surroundings can become an act of prayer, an access to the source of the something-more that draws us to these places.

The Eye of the Blackbird: How Landscapes Help Us to See God

Landscapes expose us to God's first, unmediated self-revelation. "Consider the lilies, how they grow: they neither toil nor spin; yet I tell you, even Solomon in all his glory was not clothed like one of these" (Luke 12:27; Matt 6:27-30). This brief sermon on God's loving providence for all creatures also has special relevance to our subject, for it shows the Incarnate Word reminding us that beauty is God's first self-communication. Apparently, the followers of Jesus missed that point, for centuries later Swiss theologian Hans Urs von Balthasar felt compelled to reprimand Christians for their reluctant attention to God's most neglected attribute, beauty.[8] "For life is more than food," the teaching of Jesus continues (Luke 12:23), and today, in a world divided between obesity and starvation, the admonition seems even more urgent. In the decades since Rachel Carson's *Silent Spring,* thousands of books have stridently voiced the grievances of a dying planet. With profound respect for the dedication of ecotheologians and environmental activists, I suggest that in the crusade to save the environment, ecology, poetry, and spirituality need each other.[9] Beauty argues more persuasively than guilt.

Poets and natural mystics, whose relationship with landscape can only be called *interpersonal,* notice subtle changes in light and air long before ecologists register major erosion, and those who seem immune to environmental dangers explode into action when a cherished tree or panorama is at stake. The speaker in Marilyn Robinson's narrative homily, *Gilead,* makes my point eloquently. In her novel a dying man, seeing a brief dazzle of sunlight on raindrops, exclaims:

> . . . it's easy to believe in such moments that water was made primarily for *blessing* and only secondarily for growing vegetables and doing the wash. I wish I had paid more attention to it.[10]

Extinction, or the threat of it, is making us pay attention to many such "blessings" precisely because we can no longer take them for granted. Whether we live in city, suburb, or desert, we are all surrounded by imperiled landscapes where housing projects, shopping malls, and parking lots devour field and forest, and neon jungles obliterate a firmament.

But ecological science, with its emphasis on the interdependence of all living beings in an ecosystem, demands something more concrete from us than an elegiac attachment to nature as a personification of the self. An authentic spirituality must be grounded in the natural, even when its outward expression is not activism. Fortunately, some of today's best poets are putting their special eloquence at the service of the earth.

Mary Oliver, one of the most dedicated of these, speaks as one for whom landscape is a person when she says, "I would not talk about the wind and the oak tree . . . but *on their behalf.*"[11] As prayer takes contemplatives into the mystery beyond scientific analysis, so appreciation for science confirms the value in "being nothing but the rich/Lens of attention."[12] Those who allow themselves frequent interruptions to be that lens encounter God as simultaneously transcendent and immanent. They need no ecotheology to persuade them to co-responsibility with all the other-than-human children of God with whom they share life on this planet.

Not by Bread Alone

Under the kitchen windowsill
deer tracks in the snow.
Never before have they
come so near.

No pine bough reaches down.
No signature scars the bark
or scavenges white drifts
for hidden moss.

But over there, decapitated buds
all over the azalea bush.
Premature infants
stillborn, doomed.

Mourning the glory of April
martyred in mid-winter,
we stand in strange kinship with
its ravenous assailant.

Beauty feeds on beauty.
The starving find each other
wherever we are.

Elizabeth Michael Boyle, O.P.

In this spirit of kinship, scientist John Russell calls upon Carmelite contemplatives to embrace their vocation to speak for the voiceless creatures in a universe imperiled by human greed:

> In the act of prayer, a clearer voice is given to the whole creation recapitulated through evolution and gestation in us. . . . Each cell of our body recapitulates in its genes and in its structure the entire history of life on earth.[13]

Inflections and Innuendoes: How Landscapes Call Us to Serve God

Perhaps only those whose lives are "resplendently empty"[14] can perform the service for creation that Russell assigns to Carmelites. All of us, however, can learn from and cooperate with the earthy parable through which all landscapes prefigure the redemptive death of Jesus: "Unless a grain of wheat falls into the earth and dies, it remains just a single grain; but if it dies, it bears much fruit" (John 12:24). The scientist would word it more elaborately: the grain of wheat is self-organized to die and in dying to transcend itself into something more than itself.

Even as a secular parable, the grain of wheat presents in microcosm the history of every person, civilization, and perhaps every galaxy. Few of us have met a grain of wheat "in person," but for the physical and spiritual health of all creatures, not only the wheat must die. Every forest and meadow depends for its health upon a variety of life-giving forms of death. Trees and plants die as food for animals and insects. Flowers die, scattering their seeds. Leaves, wind-pruned branches, and dead animals decompose into layers of mulch and humus that nourish roots, earthworms, microorganisms and the soil itself.[15] Nor do they die voluntarily: beneath its soil, every healthy garden is kept alive by a hidden Darwinian drama in which insects, fungi, earthworms, bacteria, and swarms of invisible insects devour each other, leaving their corpses to nourish the roots of exquisite roses. As the legendary poet-gardener Stanley Kunitz observes: "The contribution that mortality makes to civilization is the equivalent of what composting contributes to a garden. We are all candidates for composting."[16]

At the quantum level, science describes all of these processes, not as death and decomposition, but as changing forms of energy. The poet Dylan Thomas intuited this dynamic at work throughout the landscape (and within his psyche). His scientifically charged diction does not wince at our own inevitable participation in this drama:

The force that through the green fuse drives the flower
Drives my green age; that blasts the roots of trees
Is my destroyer.[17]

Unfortunately, during the past fifty years human intervention has disrupted the paschal cycle of a healthy ecosystem. Mechanized agra-business has tamed the earth's wild body and impoverished the soul of its inhabitants, while in the deserts nuclear testing inflicts unnatural death on the soil in the "garden of Allah." Unsurprisingly, many of the same people who are active in the peace movement are also ardent advocates for the environment, for the two issues are linked as early as the Book of Genesis. Here the text portrays God protesting the first mythic death-by-violence in words that anticipate the ecological impact of modern warfare: "Your brother's blood is crying out to me *from the ground!*" (Gen 4:10; italics mine).

Meantime, modern science continues to reveal many complex varieties of life-out-of-death in the continuing evolution of the universe. Today we can imagine Jesus translating the wheat grain's homily of hope into cosmic terms, both to encourage his followers and to challenge them to transformation. One of these transformative processes seems especially appropriate for reflection at this time in American and church history. Geologists tell us that new dynamic states of matter originate out of disorder, that inner disturbance causes parts to reorganize into a higher order. We call these phenomena "dissipative structures." The adjective "dissipative" describes an entity's capacity to dissipate its energies during the process of reconfiguration and transformation.[18] Wherever it occurs, this scientific phenomenon offers a striking metaphor for the sacred power operating within the universe in all of its parts. The capacity to draw good out of apparent evil, creation out of destruction, seems encoded into every landscape, even and especially into maverick malicious forces like earthquakes and volcanoes.

A scientist's description of the dissipative process reads like an account of how a civilization like ours, dying from self-inflicted consumption and corruption, just might be transformed by forces beyond its control:

> . . . if fluctuations within a system reach a critical size, they perturb the system. . . . They shake it up. The elements of the old pattern come into contact with each other in new ways and make new connections. The parts reorganize into a new whole. The system escapes into a higher order.[19]

But to those who are living through the early, destructive stages, the process feels like collapse into a lower order—or no order at all. The twenty-first century has begun with the local equivalent of a supernova explosion reverberating from Lower Manhattan to Baghdad to London to Rome, with every indication that by the time this page is published tremors will be felt on all five continents. People wonder, is this the beginning or the end of Western civilization—or both?

Here is where faith in Jesus, expanded through a cosmological perspective, can save us from both despair and complacency. A scientific perspective might give us the courage to face seriously the possibility that both American capitalist democracy and the Catholic church, as we know them, are dissipative structures in the early stages of reorganization into a higher order. Our only hope of "saving" them is to admit that they must not survive "as they are." The old Baltimore Catechism asserted confidently: "The Church as Christ founded it will last till the end of time." Clearly, a thorough dismantling of the institutional church as we know it now is needed before its holiest members can recognize "the Church as *Christ founded it*." Scientists and theologians alike urge all countercultural minorities—from parents, to pastors, to incorruptible politicians—to take heart from the behavior of dissipative structures, from their power to initiate an entirely new evolution that will dramatically change the whole behavior of the macroscopic system.[20]

Distances of time and space render most geologic revolutions invisible to the naked eye, but every once in a while a catastrophic alteration of the landscape compels our attention, and sometimes challenges our faith. Surely the tsunami of Christmas 2004 was such an event. As weeping survivors and armies of rescue workers slogged through mounds of death and debris, scientists tiptoed gingerly across the emotional landscape, reporting a process they were forced to declare "a long-range blessing for earthly life."[21] As summarized for the layman, earthquakes that trigger disastrous tidal waves are the inevitable side effect of a constant subterranean pounding geologists call "the heartbeat."

For those who believe in the resurrection, of course, death is not the worst thing that can happen, even to the young, but for the living survivors in the immediate aftermath, this is small consolation. And so the inevitable question: "Where is God in the tidal wave?" My own speculations involve more questions. What is God saying? As sacred metaphor, is the creative destruction of the tidal wave warning us that an evolving future may not include human survival—or survival of humanity as we know it? Where is God in the tidal wave? Is God buried deep in the *interiority of the event,* in a new and humbler relationship between the thoughtful survivors and the landscape with whom they have suffered and changed? Where is God in this "act of God"? Immature images of God, the benign "micro-manager" of natural and human history, cannot survive such disasters.

Where is God? Is God's only power and presence in the human response to inhuman tragedy? Something divine is almost visible in the first outpouring of human compassion, generosity, and ingenuity, but this aura of divine cooperation gradually becomes invisible in the long, hard, and humbling work of digging for new roots under the debris of scattered lives. One of the inevitable outcomes of the tsunami will be a redistribution of refugee populations, out of which new multicultural societies will eventually emerge.

> Only so, by division,
> will hope increase,
>
> like a clump of irises, which will cease to flower
> unless you distribute
> the clustered roots, unlikely source—
> clumsy and earth-covered—
> of grace.[22]

Reading geological events like tsunamis and earthquakes as parables, we note that they conform to the pattern that Paul Ricouer discerned in the parables of Jesus: orientation, disorientation, reorientation.[23] The natural world orients us to beauty and goodness as benign faces of God. Then the face turns to stone when nature becomes the enemy, a disorienting symbol of the gratuitous cruelty of divine caprice. Finally, in the work of compassion and rebuilding, we are reoriented to human responsibility, to cooperating with God in "renewing the face of the earth." A quarter-century before the great scandals of ecclesiastical authority in the American church were exposed, Catholic theologian Joseph Hallman wrote:

> One must love and hate the world; one must also love and hate the Church. One must be for destruction and creation of both, as the Bible is. And whoever does not appreciate that paradox ought not to lead in the Church.[24]

The revelations of dynamic landscapes, especially their life-affirming messages, are rarely apparent in the immediate throes of violent up-heaval. But occasionally the rescue operation itself includes a plan for the future. At the site of the Mount Saint Helen's volcanic eruption in Oregon, geologists made a historic decision not to "clean up" the place as fast as possible for the tourists. Instead, they stepped back to observe what nature herself would do to repair the landscape. The result was an astonishing demonstration of how a dissipative structure "renewed the face of the earth." In 2002, when I visited the Johnson Ridge Observation Exhibit that recorded the event and its aftermath, it struck me that Mount Saint Helen's offered both warning and hope for our embattled church, and I composed this poem as a prayer for those to whom it is addressed.

Mount Saint Helen's Delivers an Encyclical to the Institutional Church
A Found Poem

Read the Book of Earth, my brothers, shepherds of The Rock.
Listen to one who has been where you are
and now speaks out in friendship and compassion.

The largest landslide in recorded history[25]
did not come without warning.
In every historic reawakening of an uncontrollable force

there are many preliminary tremors
warning of trouble, letting off steam.
You should learn earth's language.

Hidden lava eruptions
have a Latin name: "magma."
Were you put off by its feminine gender?

This is the inside story:

Over the years *a stream of magma*
squeezed upward like toothpaste, building a dome
creating a mountain within a mountain.

Then
volcanic gases erupted for hours
reducing a forest to matchsticks
refashioning a landscape.

It was like being on the edge of an eclipse.
Then silence. Nothing but the whisper
of falling ash, like snow.

For you too now
volcanic ash has turned day to night
and eliminated all reference points.

People keep losing their bearings.
Fortunately for both of us,
that's not the whole story.

You have survived to listen, observe and learn with the faithful
as your landscape becomes like mine, a delicate, living laboratory
"God's country under construction."

Learn from my pyrotechnic parable of hope.
Within months, down my ravaged slopes
purple fireweed replaced pastures of liquid fire;

wildflowers appeared that had not existed before the blast;
new lakes glistened in sooty black craters
and thousands of elk returned.

Take heart:
already, *the first green sprouts of new growth*
appear in your ecosystem.

Plants and seeds hidden under the tight-packed snow
and small animals hibernating in underground nests and burrows
are creating beachfronts for ecological redevelopment.

Heed the Book of Earth:

Snow-capped serenity may mask turmoil
but volcanoes are as much creators as destroyers
and volcanic soils are among the world's most fertile.

With sisterly affection and concern,
I close my first encyclical
and look forward to your creative responses,
for without your action, Mother Earth tells me:
"Future eruptions are just a matter of time."

Elizabeth Michael Boyle, O.P.

Today, as destructive chaos seems to be gripping so many parts of the human community, the eyes of hope must view the ordeal as the global crucifixion that might be the destructive phase of transformation. Meantime, to Mount Saint Helen's encyclical Stanley Kunitz would add a pithy postscript:

Live in the layers,
not on the litter.[26]

NOTES

[1] Elizabeth Johnson, *Women, Earth, and Creator Spirit* (New York: Paulist Press, 1993) 27.

[2] Stanley Kunitz, *The Wild Braid: A Poet Reflects on a Century in the Garden* (New York: W. W. Norton, 2005) 61.

[3] Frederick Seidel, "The Last Remaining Angel," in *The Cosmos Poems* (New York: Farrar, Straus, and Giroux, 2000).

[4] Will Durant, cited by David Hale, "Waves of Change," *New York Times* (7 January 2005) A23.

[5] *The New Shorter Oxford English Dictionary*, vol. 1, ed. Leslie Brown (Oxford: Clarendon Press, 1993).

[6] Mircea Eliade, *Patterns in Comparative Religion* (New York: New American Library, 1958) 369; Belden Lane, *Landscapes of the Sacred: Geography and Narrative in American Spirituality* (Mahwah, NJ: Paulist Press, 1988) 17.

[7] Cited by Lynn Gamwell, *Exploring the Invisible: Art, Science, and the Spiritual* (Princeton: Princeton University Press, 2002) 28.

[8] Hans Urs von Balthasar, *The Glory of the Lord: A Theological Aesthetics*, ed. Joseph Fessio and John Riches (San Francisco: Ignatius Press, 1982–1989).

[9] Joseph Wood Krutch, a prominent foot soldier in the struggle, shares this view: "But the result may depend less upon arguments than on attitudes which are essentially emotional and aesthetic." *The Forgotten Peninsula: A Naturalist in Baja California* (Tucson: University of Arizona Press, 1986) 249.

[10] Marilyn Robinson, *Gilead* (New York: Farrar, Straus and Giroux, 2004) 27–28.

[11] Mary Oliver, *Winter Hours: Prose, Prose Poems and Poems* (New York: Houghton Mifflin, 1999) 102. Italics mine.

[12] Mary Oliver, "Entering the Kingdom," in *American Primitive* (Boston: Back Bay Books, 1983).

[13] John Russell, "Contemplation in the Vibrant Universe: The Natural Context of Christian Spirituality," in *Center for Theology and the Natural Sciences Bulletin* (Autumn 1991) 13.

[14] Mary Oliver, "White Flowers," in *New and Selected Poems* (Boston: Beacon Press, 1992).

[15] Carol Coston, *Permaculture: Finding Our Own Vines and Fig Trees* (San Antonio: Sor Juana Press, 2003) 64–69.

[16] Kunitz, *The Wild Braid*, 63.

[17] Dylan Thomas, "The Force that Through the Green Fuse Drives the Flower," in *The Poems of Dylan Thomas* (New York: New Directions, 1943).

[18] Marilyn Ferguson, *The Aquarian Conspiracy* (New York: St. Martin's Press, 1980) 12. The concept, for which Ilya Prigogine was awarded the 1977 Nobel Prize, is further elaborated in *Order Out of Chaos: Man's New Dialogue with Nature* (New York: Bantam Books, 1984).

[19] Ferguson, *The Aquarian Conspiracy*, 164–165.

[20] Prigogine, *Order Out of Chaos*, 14; Ferguson, *The Aquarian Conspiracy*, 166.

[21] William J. Broad, "Deadly and Yet Necessary, Quakes Renew the Planet," *New York Times* (11 January 2005) A1-F4.

[22] Denise Levertov, "For the New Year, 1981," in *The Life Around Us: Selected Poems on Nature* (New York: New Directions, 1997).

[23] Paul Ricouer, *Hermeneutics and the Human Sciences: Essays on Language, Action, and Interpretation,* ed. and trans. John B. Thompson (Cambridge: Cambridge University Press, 1981) 122–128.

[24] Joseph M. Hallman, "Towards a Process Theology of the Church," in *Religious Experience and Process Theology: The Pastoral Implications of a Major Modern Movement,* ed. Harry James Cargas and Bernard Lee (Mahwah, NJ: Paulist Press, 1976) 144.

[25] Italicized words are quoted or adapted from the Johnson Ridge Observation Exhibit and from Stuart Warren's essay "Eruption and Resurrection," *Portrait of Mount Saint Helen's: A Changing Landscape* (Portland, OR: Graphic Arts Center Publishing Company, 1983).

[26] Stanley Kunitz, "The Layers," in *Collected Poems* (New York: W. W. Norton, 2001).

Chapter Three

REFLECTIONS ON COSMIC EVOLUTION

". . . *The great Mother, empty yet inexhaustible . . .*
gives birth to infinite worlds . . .
always present within you."
(Lao-tzu, 551–479 B.C.)[1]

"*God created all things in such a way that*
they are not outside God. . . .
All creatures remain within God . . .
enveloped by God."
(Meister Eckhart, ca. 1260–1329)[2]

"*Blind urge had to pass over into a love that sees,*
and the clever will to possess had to be transfigured
into the foolish wisdom that pours itself out. . . .
For only love redeems."
(Hans Urs von Balthasar)[3]

"*Evolution occurs because God is more interested in adventure*
than in preserving the status quo."
(John Haught)[4]

"*In itself, the evolutionary process is*
the greatest 'proof' of a divine creative energy
at work in our world."
(Diarmuid O'Murchu)[5]

During John Paul II's final days, television screens on five continents vibrated with one colorful image: a human atlas made up of pilgrims, prelates, and heads of state from every race and major religion in the world, united in respect and gratitude for the saintly man who had seen in each and all of them the image of the God he loved. This symbol of human possibility evoked a mood of exhilaration, strange yet universal. The day before the funeral, I came upon lines that seemed written for the occasion by a blissfully emancipated scientist:

> Foreground, background. Particle and field.
> Every law that proves or justifies
> the separateness of things has been repealed . . . [6]

For me, the event seemed to render into animated metaphor Teilhard de Chardin's vision of the eschaton, the crowning stage of human evolution when all the rich variety of our species converges into a universal consciousness, the goal of "noogenesis."

In the nineteenth century, however, the first projections from evolutionary theory were not so optimistic, and indeed in the twenty-first century, evolutionary science itself seems to be an obstacle to noogenesis. From the beginning, Darwinism seemed to create a world-view dethroning God and denigrating humanity. For a while it seemed that natural history had co-opted Scripture with an explanation for *how* the world came into existence so brutal that it obsolesced all reasons *why*.

Fortunately, in the century and a half since Darwin, less conspicuous than media-exploited conflicts, a more positive attitude has developed among many theologians and thoughtful people of faith who appreciate the possibility that evolutionary science reveals God and ourselves in a warmer light than was at first supposed. For those of us who are neither scientists nor theologians, a brief summary of the highlights of evolutionary theory and some of the movements that have ensued in its wake should suffice to set the stage for reflection on how Darwinian science compels us to respect and cooperate with the mystery of a universe evolving through a combination of providence, contingency, and human freedom.

Ways of Looking: A Drama and Its Critics

In 1859 Darwin's *Origin of Species*[7] introduced a way of looking back, of tracing the biological origins of humanity to their prehistoric beginnings. Since then, Darwin's disciples have extended his vision even further backward into the eons before biology, as well as outward into the cosmos and forward in time from the Big Bang into the future. This evolutionary worldview perceives the universe, not as a completed *entity,* but as an ongoing *event.* From this it follows that existence should be described, not as a state of *being,* but as a story of *becoming.* Hence those who embrace the central tenets of Darwinian science replace the term "creation" with the phrase "the universe story." In this literary metaphor, everything in the universe, animate and inanimate, represents a paragraph, a sentence, a word in an unfinished narrative.

At least thirteen billion-plus years ago, according to present estimates, the Big Bang spewed forth the first syllables for the autobiography of the universe, that is, the indispensable chemical elements that over billions of years assembled into the conditions for organic life. During a range of 200 million to 600 million years of gradual mutation, life forms evolved from microbes to cells to organisms, early vertebrates, primates, and finally, at a date that new archeological discoveries keep adjusting almost daily, something unique occurred: a species with a capacity for abstract thought, language, and self-consciousness began to compete for control of this creative process.

Evolutionary science names no author for this astounding epic, and perhaps it is beyond the scope of science to do so. Hence by scrupulously evading characterization and plot, the tale resembles postmodern meta-fiction, simply writing itself from incoherent chaos into profound literature through the contingencies of adaptation, natural selection, and blind chance. According to evolutionary science, the force driving this completely natural phenomenon is located *within* each star, microbe, mammal that, over eons, reaches fulfillment as an aborigine, a supermodel, a Nobel laureate. Since the emergence of *homo sapiens,* the blind forces of biological evolution have slowly given way, though never completely, to cultural evolutions and revolutions dominated—and threatened—by human consciousness and choice.

This vision of the universe as an emerging rather than a static reality has profoundly influenced thought in every discipline, especially philosophy and theology. Today almost all theologians profess some form of evolutionary theism. Conservatives among them accept evolution simply as the *way* the Creator acts on matter from *within* and leave it at that. Protestant and Jewish theological progressives, however, reexamine every "article of faith" with evolution as a "given." For a long time Catholic scientists were merely "permitted" to test the theory, but a half century after Pierre Teilhard de Chardin submitted to Vatican restraints,[8] John Paul II firmly declared: ". . . evolutionary theory has been proven true. . . . we look forward to interesting discussions of theological implications."[9] This chapter will begin examining these implications, not to revise dogma, but to refresh spirituality in the light of an evolving revelation. Chapters Four and Five will probe some of the questions that evolution provokes for thoughtful Christians.

Before reflecting on the uncontested scientific premises of evolution, however, we should acknowledge the objections of two groups of people, one from the world of religion, the other from the world of science, that is, Creationists and proponents of Intelligent Design Theory. Creationism represents the extreme view of religious fundamentalists who, observing that many prominent scientists have relinquished faith in a personal God, have concluded that the only alternative to atheism is to cling tenaciously to a literal reading of Genesis. Darwin's own struggle to believe in God lends some support to their apprehension. Darwin began by declaring, "I deserve to be called a Theist,"[10] and eventually admitted, "disbelief crept over me at a slow rate, but was at last complete."[11] One need not be an atheist, however, to reject the Creationists' literalism, for a literal reading of Genesis ignores not only science but also almost two centuries of Judeo-Christian biblical scholarship.

Intelligent Design theorists, on the other hand, though allegedly neutral theologically and generally in support of some Darwinian science, are characterized by their opponents as "thinly veiled creationists." For the most part, they are credentialed scientists—physicists, chemists, and molecular-biologists—who insist that microstructural data unavailable to Darwin disprove the process of natural selection and argue for the necessity of intelligence and design in the origin and development of the universe.[12] Intelligent Design Theory (IDT) appeals to the logic of many educated people—professing varying levels of theism and agnosticism—who find it intellectually difficult to accommodate "the Myth of the Great Accident" or, like the poet Mary Oliver, emotionally impossible to "live through one day believing nothing is significant, nothing is governed by the unknowable, the divine."[13] No less a scientist than Einstein expressed sentiments similar to the poet's: "That deeply emotional conviction of the presence of a superior reasoning power, which is revealed in the incomprehensible universe, forms my idea of God."[14]

This debate, which shows no sign of abating, prompted Stephen Jay Gould to quip: "The demise of Darwinism has been trumpeted more often than the guard change at Buckingham Palace."[15] (One could say the same of theism.) Eighty years to the day after John Scopes was arrested for teaching evolution in Tennessee, parents in twenty American states, with support from Intelligent Design scientists, assembled in court to demand the right of science teachers to give equal time in their curricula to both neo-Darwinian "dogma" and its challengers in the scientific community.[16] This legal action attracted wider media attention than any other case before the state court and set in motion a year-long preoccupation with evolution in the American press, prompting articles by columnists and cartoonists whose usual specialties were politics and entertainment.[17]

Though scientists and popes from Pius XII to Benedict XVI insist that evolution is a description of a physical process, outside the realm of metaphysical and theological speculation, the issue continues to be framed as a contest between urbane scientists and emotional religionists.[18] Yet some proponents and adversaries defy stereotypes. For example, Nobel Laureate Francis Crick, co-discoverer of DNA structure, goes so far as to expostulate: "Theories of undirected origins of life are as credible as the notion that space aliens sent a rocket ship to the earth to seed it with spores," while microbiologist Lynne Margulis predicts that history will ultimately judge neo-Darwinism itself "a minor twentieth-century religious sect within the sprawling religious persuasion of Anglo-Saxon biology."[19]

John Paul II's 1996 statement, cited above, has been widely invoked as a Roman Catholic endorsement of neo-Darwinism. In fact, the church rejects equally the extremes of both a literal reading of Genesis and the exclusion of a Creator from the evolutionary process. In his first homily as pope, Benedict XVI directly reassured his faith community: "We are not some casual and meaningless product of evolution. Each of us is willed, each of us is loved, each of us is necessary."[20]

As evolution continued to make news in American courts, Cardinal Christoph Schönborn, O.P., lead editor of the 1992 *Catechism of the Catholic Church,* published what was obviously intended to be a brief clarification of the Roman Catholic position on the subject. Catholic doctrine is based, Cardinal Schönborn argues, not on a literal reading of Genesis, but on an appeal to human reason. "Any system of thought that denies or seeks to explain away the overwhelming evidence for design in biology is ideology, not science."[21] Cardinal Schönborn cites a similar statement by John Paul II in which he condemns talk of blind chance as equivalent to an abdication of human intelligence and, by extension, of responsibility for human problems.[22] Cardinal Schönborn does not cite his fellow Dominican, Thomas Aquinas, who characteristically includes both providence and chance in his view of the creative process: "It would be contrary to the nature of providence and to the perfection of the world, if nothing happened by chance."[23]

Although far from clarifying the Catholic position, Cardinal Schönborn's piece elicited comment from Catholic scientists and theologians that demonstrated an interesting variety of nuanced beliefs. Most of them expressed considerable distress that the cardinal seemed to be promoting Intelligent Design Theory, for which they as scientists had little respect.[24] Unfortunately, since some of the cardinal's arguments seemed to be citations from publications of The Discovery Institute, a Republican-supported think tank, Cardinal Schönborn found himself in the eye of the political hurricane whirling around the "faith-based" administration of American President George Bush. Hence, when the *New York Times* issued a series of articles on the controversy, the first piece was devoted almost entirely to the political affiliations of Intelligent Design theorists and their financial supporters.[25]

On July 12, 2005, three prominent American Catholic biology professors published "An Open Letter to Benedict XVI" requesting that he issue a prompt "clarification" consistent with previous Vatican statements on evolution. Anticipating a long wait for a reply, perhaps, one of the signators, Kenneth R. Miller of Brown University, published his own, entitled "Darwin, Design, and the Catholic Faith." With copious reference to popes, scientists, and theologians, he reassured the faithful and the public that the cardinal was expressing an opinion, not a dogma; that the church does not endorse Creationism; that "true contingency is not incompatible with a purposeful divine providence"; and that neo-Darwinism is not necessarily incompatible with belief in God.[26] Benedict's exposition, when and if it comes, can scarcely be more reassuring.

The controversy brought to wide public attention a strong undercurrent in religious academia. For some time, some progressive Christian theologians have shifted positions, largely unnoticed by the pedestrian churchgoer, from defending religion against science to defending both science and religion from fundamentalism. Surprisingly, these theologians are choosing to describe Darwinism as more *theologically* appealing than Intelligent Design Theory. As a result, even within mainstream churches, definitions of "God" now vary widely—and are rarely conspicuous for clarity.

Among opponents of IDT, the most creative, perhaps, is Catholic theologian John Haught, director of the Georgetown Center for the Study of Science and Religion. Haught focuses, not on the case for "intelligence," but on the case against "design." His many pages devoted to carefully reasoned objections to IDT persuasively challenge "design" as a form of "predestination," a doctrine to which Catholicism has long been opposed.[27] Haught explains that the concept of an eternally-ordained design "ironically limits the designer."[28] "From a biblical perspective," Haught continues, "God must be thought of, after all, as the inexhaustible—but sometimes disquieting—wellspring of novelty and not as an imagined source of fixed order."[29] Haught's view corresponds with that expressed by Teilhard de Chardin half a century earlier: "God has voluntarily limited his omniscience and omnipotence in order to endow creation with freedom. Freedom is a divine gift, and its range increases as evolution proceeds."[30] Teilhard's statement, which implicitly rejects the *control* inherent in a pre-ordained *design,* does specify a divine *purpose:* "in order to endow creation with freedom."

At this point I suggest that the safest position for the Christian non-specialist is to be guided by a vision of evolution in which God is neither micromanager nor absentee landlord, but present in the universe and in human freedom and creativity as *empowerment.* This empowering presence of God mirrors the *experience* of God in our lives: a combination of loving providence, capricious nature, and free response—or resistance—to love. Open to the revelations of science evolving almost daily, we can be especially attentive to those that call us to deeper faith and responsibility. Reading science in tandem with spiritual literature, beginning with Scripture and continuing through Christian mystics from Eckhart to Teilhard and contemporary "panentheists," I have found that the act of faith, like the act of creation, "does not fade into the past but *is always in the beginning and in process and new.*"[31] Whether or not our individual faith experience concurs with all the conclusions of evolutionary theists, the insights of these explorers can gradually lead us to a more mature relationship with God. From among all their speculations, I have selected a few that I have found challenging.

The Eye of the Blackbird: The Evolutionist Looks at God

One of the first scholars to extrapolate the spiritual implications of evolution was the metaphysician Alfred North Whitehead.[32] Whitehead had a genius for taking both sides of an argument and proving both true. His "process theology"[33] insists that Divine Love is primordial, abstract, and changeless, the timeless ground of all possibility, and at the same time, concrete, moving, in process.[34] The snowy mountains in Wallace Stevens' landscape seem an appropriate image for Whitehead's God, who only *seems* to be still and changeless but is actually "in process." In the very becoming of the universe, process theologians claim, God also becomes. Whitehead might designate our moving blackbird as human longing and the mountain range as God, "the poet of the world, with tender patience leading it by his vision of truth, beauty, and goodness."[35] For me, the dual image of bird and mountain captures more accurately the duality of our experience of God, a presence sometimes serene, solid, soaring impassively "above it all," at others an abstract idea, fickle, elusive, moving out of range, mocking faith's need for mental and emotional footholds. The latter seems to be the operative imagery at this time in human history, when thoughtful believers are struggling to incorporate scientific advances into their relationships with God and with the world.

How, specifically, does evolutionary thinking affect these relationships? The first consequences are profoundly personal, and therefore invisible to others. To begin with, our embrace of evolutionary science emancipates God from the limitations of our old spatial imagery and should eliminate from our thought and conversation all references to God as "up above" or "out there." Evolution assures us that God is not an extraterrestrial. Envisioning God *within* the evolving universe empowers a deep intimacy with a Creator Spirit who is truly everywhere. The feelings expressed in the familiar poetry of the psalmist assume a new dynamism:

> Where can I go from your spirit?
> > Or where can I flee from your presence?
> If I ascend to heaven, you are there;
> > if I make my bed in Sheol, you are there.
> If I take the wings of the morning
> > and settle at the farthest limits of the sea
> even there your hand shall lead me
> > and your right hand shall hold me fast (Ps 139:7-10).

Defining evolution as God's active presence in everything that exists can open us to the mystics' experience of "wholeness" and of "presence." Gradually, "a process philosophy of religion . . . based primarily in religious experience,"[36] becomes a "homepage" within us with links to a web of ecumenical, feminist, and liberation theologies.

Although some contemporary scientists and theologians have moved technically beyond the thought of Teilhard de Chardin, no mystic of modern times offers a more dramatic model of a scientifically inspired spirituality than he does. Beginning at a very young age, Teilhard experienced physical matter itself as the locus of "a fire like that of the burning bush," "the Diaphany of the Divine at the heart of the glowing universe."[37] Like almost all mystics, Teilhard struggled with pantheism and ultimately concluded:

> . . . pantheism is only the defective expression of a well-justified (and moreover, ineradicable) tendency in the human soul . . . to recognize the importance . . . of the Whole. . . . Man is drawn towards the One . . . not by his reason alone, but by the full force of his whole being. . . . Parallel with (and in a sense identical with) our intellectual need for *unity,* we experience, deep within us, an affective and spontaneous need for *union.*[38]

All mystics achieve this affective union, not with God-in-things (pantheism), but with all things in God (panentheism). Theistic evolution is a scientific metaphor, affirming Christianity's earliest eco-theology, the recognition of a vibrant invisible reality "in whom we live and move and have our being" (Acts 17:28). For this reason, scientists Philip Clayton and Sir Arthur Peacocke chose this biblical phrase as the title for the published papers of their 2001 symposium on panentheism. At this international and ecumenical colloquium, scientists and theologians synthesized panentheistic thinking from the pre-Christian Hindu scriptures to familiar theologians of all faiths in our current century.[39]

The second spiritual impact of evolutionary thinking manifests itself at the practical level in an intensified sense of responsibility for the world around us. One obvious example of a practical outcome is the energetic partnership between scientists and religionists in the movement for environmental justice. The ecological crisis of our time has made science and theology "companions in tribulation," facing a common adversary, "the nihilism practiced in our dealings with nature."[40]

Following a theological tradition at least as old as Augustine,[41] biblical scholars have reinterpreted Genesis in the light of science to replace a relationship of *domination* over the natural world with one of *kinship*.[42] Eco-feminists and eco-theologians tell us that renouncing our feeling of superiority to all other beings constitutes the first step toward environmental justice. Of course, poets have long enjoyed kinship with beasts and flowers; they are now happy to accept scientific endorsement for an attitude that was once regarded as playful or eccentric. "After all," says Stanley Kunitz stroking a garden snake, "we are partners in this land, co-signers of a covenant."[43]

Like all intimate relationships, kinship with the "other-than-human" can be a revelatory event. In the infinite variety of creation, God has provided companions to suit every temperament. For scientists and poets of a certain temperament, light itself can become a person.

Release

"Matter is nothing but gravitationally-trapped light." (David Bohm)

Approaching ninety, the Nobel poet
sees all his former lives and landscapes
returning home to him
wearing "the clarity of early morning."[44]

Such grace for me belongs
to winter afternoons when
sudden incandescent candor
limns each naked tree

exposing all so gently that
I hear myself declaring:
"You know me as no one
has ever known me."

This is the hour when light
arriving late as usual
becomes the generous wedding guest
who saves the best wine

until now
when mountains, roofs, and rooted things
set free their trapped transparency
and strip us to our own.

Elizabeth Michael Boyle, O.P.

Kinship among all inhabitants of the planet seems to have been intuited in our language even before it became "official" science. The very etymology of the word *ecology,* "doctrine of the house," derives from a theological view of creation as the *house of God.*[45] In this house all creatures live as a family whose health depends upon cooperation among its members. Kinship and familial cooperation are a long way, however, from Darwin's "survival of the fittest." Since 1967, eminent microbiologist Lynn Margulis has been able to provide evidence for a "kinder gentler" hypothesis. At the molecular level, Margulis has demonstrated to the satisfaction of skeptics that new microscopic species develop, not by way of Darwinian competition, but by way of *symbiotic* relationships.[46]

Long before technology gave molecular biologists the equipment to demonstrate such a process at the microscopic level, Teilhard had advanced the notion of biological symbiosis and imagined human social evolution modeled on it. According to Teilhard, the symbiotic process that produced creatures of increasing complexity early in evolutionary history "is continuing today, and even accelerating, not primarily in the biosphere, but in the sphere of consciousness . . . drawing mankind into a unified whole."[47] During his lifetime Teilhard's concept was discarded as far-fetched, and indeed, not even the reality of global electronic "symbiosis" via the Internet embodies the full force of his bold vision. This is the vision for which the international/interfaith assembly in St. Peter's Square, with which this chapter opened, offers hope.

Inflections and Innuendoes
Evolution as an Advent Experience

"Evolution is not a mere hypothesis, but a condition of all experience," says Teilhard.[48] In its annual liturgical cycle, the Christian church acts out a ritual drama of human experience, both cyclical and evolving, a pattern I hope to demonstrate in this and subsequent chapters, where we will reflect on scientific metaphors for the liturgical seasons.

Of all the connections between evolution and religious belief, none feels more familiar to me than the image of God as the future toward which everything in the universe yearns. Every Advent we experience God as a promise that grows toward fulfillment in us, as a child grows in the womb. At the same time, in the back of our minds lies a perennial paradox: Jesus came two thousand years ago and has never left us; he comes again and again in the Word, in the sacraments, in prayer. Why, then, do we begin each liturgical year begging him to come and, in fact, often experience simultaneously both the divine absence and its mysteriously new arrival? Because, evolutionary theology explains, God is, by definition, that which is ahead, beyond, "the future that forever faithfully takes us and our world into itself where resides the really real. . . ."[49] According to Haught, this understanding of divine transcendence corresponds closely to the God of the Bible, who, in passage after Old Testament passage, *goes before* the people, leading them to liberty.[50] Profoundly interpreted, evolution leads to "a metaphysics of promise"[51] in which the purpose of the universe itself is to be the revelatory Scripture, gradually unfolding the reality of what "can be only vaguely visualized in metaphor, symbol and myth."[52]

The understanding that comes so slowly to scientists and theologians comes to poets in intuitive flashes by way of metaphors that retain the mystery they illuminate. One such extended metaphor for all that has been said above is Samuel Beckett's classic *Waiting for Godot*. Scholarly speculation on the identity of Godot fills volumes, since the long-awaited offstage presence never arrives to explain itself. Hence critics have variously identified Godot as truth, human desire, or the future—whatever is always coming, but never here. If we knew who Godot is, if we could name him, we would no longer be waiting. But because Godot has promised to come, Didi and Gogo wait, systematically discarding all inadequate words for the Unnamable for whom they keep vigil. Everyone in the darkened theater of the world waits with them.

Secular Darwinian critics would insist that Didi and Gogo represent the folly of believers waiting for life's ultimate meaning. But waiting in hope, trusting in the promise of a future beyond all human understanding, makes the bleakest existence meaningful. Years ago Samuel Beckett's most renowned interpreter, Jack McGowran, gave a performance at the college where I teach. Afterward, when students engaged him in conversation, one of them commented: "Beckett understands our despair." Instantly, McGowran protested: "No, no, not despair;

Beckett is always about *hope*. Beckett *defines* man as the creature who can't stop hoping." Honoring this testimony from an actor who had literally inhabited Beckett for decades, I have always subtitled *Waiting for Godot:* "The Existentialist's Advent."

A promising God, "who opens up the world to the future, is the ultimate explanation of the universe."[53] Every Advent, faith takes us deeper into this mystery: our God *has come* and *is coming*. God has been revealed in the metaphors of creation, of Scripture, of history, and in the person of Jesus Christ. But God's self-communication is not limited to the religious dogmas constructed to accommodate our closed and inadequate understanding of these revelations. The God of the promise for whom Abraham and his children are still waiting, the God of Isaiah for whose peaceable kingdom our war-torn planet is still longing, the God to whom Jesus prayed "that all may be one"—this is the God, both revealed and concealed in all metaphors, who is here and is still coming, and therefore, "abides in the world most intimately in the mode of promise."[54]

Advent liturgies voice more than the spirit of a season; they echo what St. Paul heard as "the groaning of all creation" (Rom 8:23). In verses of layered metaphor, one poet encounters synonyms for the scientist's craving for knowledge expressed as "design" in everything from the potholes of Manhattan to the interplanetary "black holes" of outer space.

Design
"It is the dumb hunger, thrust upon the world." (Robert Haas)

I remember the mountain mined of limestone
a white womb flooded with rain
how the quarry deep and blue grew
out of the empty. Birds came
and deer with their shy thirst.

Holes in the earth have always drawn me
a swath of mystery rooted in the ground . . .
canyons carved by boiling rivers
the desert honed like a massive bowl
by a meteorite flung from orbit.

Once on the island of Santorini
I watched the natives emerge from a pit
as if ascending from water
carrying buckets of sand pail by pail
a stone village buried in time.

There are holes buried in Manhattan
pocking the landscape like gypsies
predicting the concrete future
and rabbits sculpting a warren
under a grassy ceiling in my yard.

Each winter I watch snow
pile itself on the hillside
fill each pore and aperture of earth
like grace it drifts
all blue white and dazzling.

They say in the galaxies
gravity is so dense
light waves bend
creating a black hole with no end
and who among us can resist the pull

of the great yawning holes in knowledge
always this yearning
to fill.

Marion Goldstein

Scientists hope to track down and grasp ultimate reality. People of faith hope to be found and grasped by that affective knowledge, inaccessible to mere intellect, that comes to the poor in spirit through simple communion. Every Advent the church invites us to prepare for the fulfillment of hope by cleansing hope itself. As T. S. Eliot, echoing John of the Cross, urges: "Wait without hope, for hope would be hope for the wrong thing," until "the faith and the love and the hope are all in the waiting."[55] The following prayer illustrates the way that reflecting on evolution as metaphor can open the way to such communion.

Trinity

If what I believe is true
    the entire universe was and is
    being created in you.

As a mother makes room
    for her child within her womb
    so you make room for me within you.

You, O Triune God of mutual relations
    and reciprocal arrangements,
    come as well and dwell within me.

And when you enter my being
    you bring the universe with you
Miracle enough that you come.
Now all that has been created
    and you Three live in me.

No wonder I feel
    the pulse of the moon
    the heartbeat of the earth
    the synergy of the wind
    the cry of the poor
    tugging at my heart.
All is within me.
All is within you.
    So intimately connected we.

Mary McGuinness, O.P.

The poet wrote her prayer after reading *The God of Evolution* by Denis Edwards.[56] Half a century ago I came upon a similar meditation by John of the Cross. I remember being so inspired by it that I repeated it to a priest in a summary something like this: "Everything that exists is in God and God is in me. So, the sun, the moon, and the stars are also in me, the mountains and oceans, forests and flowers, angels and saints, and the Mother of God are all in God and therefore in me." Unimpressed, my holy advisor remonstrated: "If God is in you, what do you need with all this other stuff?" While I no longer hesitate to join

St. John in celebrating the sacredness of "all this other stuff," I hope it includes the "cry of the poor," which the sixteenth-century saint left out. Theology itself is evolving, as it always has. Even for John of the Cross, there's always hope for improvement. That hope is the theme of the next poem.

Under Construction

"They're not dead yet,"
my mother used to say
whenever friends or neighbors gushed:
"How proud you must be
of your children."

"They're not dead yet."
To herself more than others she addressed
this Irish-Catholic version of "knock wood,"
her proleptic antidote to the Gospel caveat:
"Whoever exalts herself shall be humbled."

Generations later
to baffled and despairing elders
I echo her once-amusing mantra
stripped of superstition
and redolent of hope:

"Don't worry. They're not dead yet:
your sullen, unrecognizable offspring—,
unrepentant slayers of parental expectation.
They're still in process
as you and I and all our promises and prayers are."

Through light years of yearning
the voice of a universe,
parent of us, all speaks clearly:
"I am Who Am
the One Who is to come."

"Come what may, I am still coming.
Trust in them as I trust you
to emerge from this creative chaos.
Patience.
We're not dead yet."

Elizabeth Michael Boyle, O.P.

NOTES

[1] Lao-tzu, *Tao Te Ching: A New English Version by Stephen Mitchell* (New York: Harper and Row, 1988) 6.

[2] Matthew Fox, trans., *Meditations with Meister Eckhart: A Centering Book* (Santa Fe: Bear and Co., 1983) 22.

[3] Hans Urs Von Balthasar, "Heart of the World," in Erasmo S. Lavia, trans., *Magnificat*, vol. 6, no. 5 (July 2004) 142–143.

[4] John Haught, *God after Darwin: A Theology of Evolution* (Boulder, CO: Westview Press, 2000) 42.

[5] Diarmuid O'Murchu, *Quantum Theology: Spiritual Implications of the New Physics* (New York: Crossroad, 2003) 59.

[6] Marilyn L. Taylor, "One by One," in *Subject to Change* (WordTech Communications, 2004).

[7] Charles Darwin, *On the Origin of Species by Means of Natural Selection or Preservation of Favored Races in the Struggle for Life* (London: Murray, 1859).

[8] The Jesuit paleontologist lived from 1881 to 1955. His scientific works, suppressed during his lifetime, were published posthumously.

[9] John Paul II, "Message to the Pontifical Academy of Sciences on Evolution," 22 October 1996. *Origins* (14 November 1996) 352.

[10] *Life and Letters of Charles Darwin,* ed. F. Darwin (New York: D. Appleton, 1887), in *Creationism vs. Evolution,* ed. Bruno J. Leone (San Diego: Greenhaven Press, 2002) 76.

[11] Charles Darwin, *The Autobiography of Charles Darwin,* ed. Nora Barlow (New York: W. W. Norton, 1993) 85.

[12] For example, Michael Behe, *Darwin's Black Box: The Biochemical Challenge to Evolution* (New York: Simon and Schuster, 1996); William Dembski, *Intelligent Design: The Bridge Between Science and Theology* (Downer's Grove, IL: InterVarsity Press, 1999); and numerous others cited by Behe and Dembski.

[13] Mary Oliver, "Sand Dabs Four," in *Winter Hours Prose, Prose Poems and Poems* (Boston: Mariner Books, 2004).

[14] Albert Einstein, quoted in *The Hand of God: Thoughts and Images Reflecting the Spirit of the Universe,* ed. Michael Reagan (Philadelphia: Templeton Foundation Press, 1999) 32.

[15] Stephen Jay Gould, *The Structure of Evolutionary Theory* (Cambridge: The Belknap Press of Harvard University Press, 2002) 585.

[16] Jodi Wilgoren, "In Kansas, Darwinism Goes On Trial Once More," *New York Times* (5 May 2005) A18; Cornelia Dean, "Opting Out in the Debate on Evolution," *New York Times* (21 June 2005) F1.

[17] For example, Elizabeth Bumiller, Washington correspondent; Paul Krugman, political columnist; William Safire, language maven; John Schwartz, film critic. See Works Cited at the back of this volume.

[18] Stephen Jay Gould makes the case for what he calls "Non-Overlapping Magesteria" in *Rocks of Ages: Science and Religion in the Fullness of Life* (New York: Ballantine Books, 1999).

[19] Francis Crick, cited in "The Evolution of the Skeptic: An Interview with Michael Behe," http://www.origins.org/mc/resources/behe/html. Lynn Margulis, quoted in "Lynn Margulis: Science's Unruly Earth Mother," *Science Magazine*, no. 252, 378.

[20] Benedict XVI, homily at papal installation, 25 April 2005, quoted by Christoph Schönborn, "Finding Design in Nature," *New York Times* (7 July 2005) A23.

[21] Schönborn, "Finding Design in Nature."

[22] Ibid.

[23] *Summa Contra Gentiles*, III.74.

[24] John C. Allen, Jr. "Catholic Experts Urge Caution in Evolution Debate," *National Catholic Reporter* (29 July 2005) 5–7.

[25] Jodi Wilgoren, "Politicized Scholars Put Evolution on the Defensive," *New York Times* (8 August 2005) A1. The *Times* series was obviously inspired, not by an interest in "pure science," but by the steady intrusion of politics into science education throughout the nation. For example, Elizabeth Bumiller, "Bush Remarks Roil Debate on Teaching Evolution," *New York Times* (3 August 2005); David Stout, "Frist Urges Two Teachings on Life Origins," *New York Times* (20 August 2005).

[26] Kenneth R. Miller, "Darwin, Design, and the Catholic Faith." http://www.millerandlevine.com/km/evol, 19 September 2005.

[27] Haught, *God after Darwin*, 17.

[28] John Haught, *Deeper than Darwin: The Prospect for Religion in the Age of Evolution* (Boulder, CO: Westview Press, 2003) 131.

[29] Ibid.

[30] Pierre Teilhard de Chardin, quoted by Theodosius Dobzhansky in "Teilhard de Chardin and the Orientation of Evolution," *Process Theology: Basic Writings by Key Thinkers of a Major Modern Movement*, ed. Ewert H. Cousins (New York: Newman Press, 1971) 245.

[31] Meister Eckhart, *Breakthrough: Meister Eckhart's Creation Spirituality in a New Translation*, trans. Matthew Fox (New York: Image Books, 1980) 111.

[32] Alfred North Whitehead (1861–1947). The influence of his *Process and Reality*, published in 1929, can be seen in virtually all contemporary scholars in the science-religion community.

[33] Various expressions of "process theology" can be traced at least as far back as Buddhism, as Charles Hartshorne has demonstrated. "The Development of Process Theology," *Process Theology*, 47–66.

[34] Charles Hartshorne, "Whitehead's Idea of God," *Whitehead's Philosophy* (Lincoln: University of Nebraska Press, 1972) 63–97.

[35] Alfred North Whitehead, *Process and Reality: An Essay in Cosmology* (New York: Macmillan, 1960) 526.

[36] David Ray Griffen, *Reenchantment without Supernaturalism: A Process Philosophy of Religion* (Ithaca, NY: Cornell University Press, 2001) 10.

[37] Teilhard's autobiography, *The Heart of Matter,* trans. Ursula King (London: Collins, 1978) 16.

[38] Teilhard de Chardin, *Christianity and Evolution,* trans. Rene Hague (New York: Harcourt Brace Jovanovich, 1971) 56–57. See also Teilhard's essay "Pantheism and Christianity."

[39] Philip Clayton and Arthur Peacocke, eds., *In Whom We Live and Move and Have Our Being: Panentheistic Reflections on God's Presence in a Scientific World,* (Grand Rapids: Eerdmans, 2004).

[40] Jürgen Moltmann, *God in Creation: A New Theology of Creation and the Spirit of God* (New York: Harper and Row, 1985) 34.

[41] Torricius van Bavel, "The Creator and the Integrity of Creation in the Fathers of the Church," *Augustinian Studies* 21 (1990) 1–33.

[42] Elizabeth Johnson, *Women, Earth, and Creator Spirit* (New York: Paulist Press, 1993).

[43] Stanley Kunitz, "Snakes of September," in *Collected Poems* (New York: W. W. Norton, 2000).

[44] Czeslaw Milosz, "Late Ripeness," in *Second Space: New Poems* (New York: HarperCollins, 2004).

[45] Jürgen Moltmann, *God in Creation,* xii–xiii. Moltmann, one of Europe's leading Protestant theologians, is credited with introducing into mainstream theological discourse terms that now pervade American ecotheology: *indwelling, participating, mutuality.*

[46] Lynn Margulis, http://www.geo.umass.edu/faculty/margulis. Richard Dawkins, ordinarily an adversary, was forced to admire Margulis for "the courage and stamina to carry her radical theory to orthodoxy." Online http://www. Edge .org/documents. Third Culture/n.-Ch 7.html.

[47] Summarized by Ewert H. Cousins in *Process Theology,* 17.

[48] Quoted by Ursula King, 36.

[49] Haught, *Deeper than Darwin,* 128.

[50] Haught, *God after Darwin,* 39.

[51] Haught, *Deeper than Darwin,* 128.

[52] Ibid., 144.

[53] Ibid., 128.

[54] Ibid., 144.

[55] T. S. Eliot, "East Coker," in *The Complete Poems and Plays* (New York: Harcourt, Brace and Company, 1952).

[56] Denis Edwards, *The God of Evolution: A Trinitarian Theology* (New York and Mahwah, NJ: Paulist Press, 1999).

Chapter Four

REFLECTIONS ON DIVINE AND HUMAN SUFFERING

"A star blazed in my womb."
(Makida, Queen of Sheba, ca. 1000 B.C.E.)[1]

"From the first instant, the universe is pregnant with life."
(Christian de Duve, Nobel Chemist, 1995)[2]

"Now I will cry out like a woman in labor, gasping and panting."
(Isaiah 42:14)

"God waits on history and suffers as she waits."
(Meister Eckhart, ca. 1260–1329)[3]

"And you are the beneficiaries of all that struggle for light,
heir to all that agony. . . . Every human being has a responsibility
to all those creatures whose agony and groaning
have given him birth."
(Donald Nicholl, 1987)[4]

"Nothing is lost, nothing created, everything is transformed."
(Antoine de Lavoisier, 1789)[5]

"You who batter us and then dress our wounds,
you who resist us and yield to us,
you who wreck and build, shackle and liberate . . .
I acclaim you as the divine milieu."
(Pierre Teilhard de Chardin, 1955)[6]

"The prohibition against images of God seeks to safeguard the ultimate transcendence of God . . . the fact that God cannot be manipulated."[7] Yet humanity, often well-intentioned, continues trying to do just that—to impose upon God the reverse image of our own inadequacies. It takes a "radical" re-imaging of God, which seems at first iconoclastic, to retrieve the true face intuited by ancient wisdom. When such a "new" paradigm is announced, the event often elicits from people of faith a sigh of relieved recognition: "I've always wanted to think of God that way, but was afraid to say so."

Such is the case with the "new orthodoxy"[8] of a suffering God. In fact, the stone-faced God whom Darwin dethroned never really existed. That God resembles more closely the faceless natural force that atheist Richard Dawkins adores: "Nature is neither kind nor unkind . . . neither against suffering nor for it . . . unless it affects the survival of DNA."[9] The pre-Darwinian deity, a mythological being, perfect in power and impervious to pain, although still popular with some triumphal sects, was, is, and ever shall be incompatible with the "vulnerable" God who spoke to the prophets and continues to speak through our poets:

> We must not portray you in king's robes,
> you drifting mist that brought forth the morning.
>
> Once again from the old paintboxes
> we take the same gold for scepter and crown
> that has disguised you through the ages.
>
> Piously we produce our images of you
> till they stand around you like a thousand walls.
> And when our hearts would simply open,
> our fervent hands hide you.[10]
>
> *Rainer Maria Rilke*

Is it not the holy compassion of a God who suffers that shone through the battered body of Jesus Christ, who "emptied himself," becoming obedient to the forces of history (Phil 2:8)? Some scientific theologians now envision a prehistoric cosmic kenosis in which the creator emptied divine power into all the chaos and contingency of the universe. Hence process theology envisions God as "the great companion of all human experience . . . the fellow sufferer who understands."[11]

Evolutionary science obsolesces the picture of an external force exercising perfect dominion over a universe. In the view of scientific theists, that kind of total control is a burden our freedom-loving God gladly incinerated in the fires of the Big Bang. Hence, "Darwin's gift to theology"[12] relieves believers of an impossible task: reconciling divine power with the scandal of human suffering. As gradually as the incremental mutations in Darwinian evolution itself, many Christian theologians have transformed respectful but distorted descriptions of the deity. The changeless one who presides with imperturbable calm over all earthly anguish has yielded to a "crucified God" who shares profoundly in all agonies. Evolutionary science is the starting point for a series of independent movements that eventually converge in the concept of a God who suffers not only with men and women but with the earth itself.

Although a few Catholic theologians have mounted learned protests against this "new orthodoxy," John Paul II himself declared: "God enters into human and cosmic suffering which will redeem the world."[13] Each liturgical year, in the same way that the evolutionary concept of the "one who is coming" can orient us toward a fresh experience of Advent, so, too, meditation with our suffering God can prepare us for a profound experience of Lent. The following summary deliberately leaves to professional scientists and theologians the technical hairsplitting that is their legitimate concern. Our focus will be limited to provisional insights from science conducive to cultivating an adult spirituality.

A Way of Looking: From the Prophets to Liberation Theology

Three major factors contributed to the steady emergence of a theology of divine suffering: biblical scholarship, the influence of process thought, and the "problem of God" in relation to global human suffering (especially genocide). Though these developments were simultaneous, we will consider them here sequentially. From the perspective of biblical spirituality, theologians of all faiths acknowledge that the most influential contribution to the conversation came from Rabbi Abraham Heschel's classic *The Prophets*.[14] In this exposition of his "doctrine of the divine pathos," Heschel is concerned with neither philosophy nor theology, but with God's self-communication through a direct relationship with humanity. With sensitivity and passion, Heschel explores the *experience* of the prophets with a living God who interacts with human history and responds to human behavior and desire: "This notion that God . . . possesses, not merely intelligence and will, but also pathos, basically defines the prophetic consciousness of God, . . . [which] finds its deepest expression in the fact that God can actually suffer."[15]

Heschel traces and interprets pervasive expressions of God's sorrow, disappointment, weariness, and grief throughout the Old Testament, and carefully points out how divine suffering differs from ours:

My heart recoils within me;
>   my compassion grows warm and tender.
I will not execute my fierce anger . . .
>   for I am a God and no mortal (Hos 11:8).

Fully conscious of the danger of anthropomorphism, Heschel comments:

> The divine pathos combining absolute selflessness with supreme concern for the poor and the exploited can hardly be regarded as the attribution of human characteristics. Where is the man endowed with such characteristics? . . . Divine pathos is a genuine insight into God's relatedness to man, rather than a projection of human traits into divinity . . . as in the god images of mythology.[16]

Any reader whose faith feels chilled when scientists/theologians refine their definitions of God into cool abstractions should re-read Heschel once a year (or once a week if necessary). In the experience of the prophets, says the rabbi, God emerges as "all-personal, all-subject,"[17] the very antithesis of detachment.[18]

Heschel's compelling work on God's self-communication through the prophets can be read as a plea to modern scholars not to follow the Pied Piper of sophistication into the mountain pass of impersonality. As we know, such intellectual seduction eventuated in the oxymoronic "Death of God" theology of the sixties. For other scholars, however, Darwinian science engendered a vision of God that closely resembles Heschel's God of the prophets. In the light of evolution, "process theology"[19] challenges the notion of a stable, unchanging, totally detached God and suggests instead a God who is intimately connected with the unfolding "process" not only of creation, but also of human history.[20] Like Rabbi Heschel, process theologians are careful to note how divine suffering differs from ours. "God feels what we feel, but not as we feel it, that is, not as God's pain but as ours."[21] God not only suffers *with* us but *for* us when we ourselves feel no pain. A good example would be when Jesus lamented over Jerusalem because of his people's missed opportunities for intimacy. Such evolutionary theology makes practical demands on us. We read the morning newspaper with its scenes of brutality and degradation and cry out, "Where is God?" With Jesus Christ, contemporary theology replies, "God is here, *in redemptive agony, waiting for you to act.*"

Finally, it is clear that theologians developed the concept of a suffering God not only in intellectual response to science but more urgently in moral response to the global enormity of physical pain in our time. John Haught deliberately raises the question in relation to science: "How could a powerful and compassionate God permit all the agony, aimless wandering, and waste that scientific portrayals of evolution have laid out for us?"[22] In the face of the unprecedented human atrocities of current history, we voice variations of the same question more passionately. After Auschwitz, Rwanda, Darfur, Iraq, only two positions are possible: either a God of love does not exist, or God who is love is not exempt from suffering. As poet Archibald MacLeish expressed the logical options:

> If God is God, He is not good,
> If God is good, He is not God.
> Take the even, take the odd,
> I would not sleep here if I could. . . .[23]

Holocaust survivor Elie Wiesel came to the first conclusion in the often-cited scene from *Night* where a young man watching a child hanged declares: "God died on that tree."[24] Reinterpreting the scene, Jürgen Moltmann uses the same words to say, "God died on that tree. The inexpressible sufferings of Auschwitz were also the sufferings of God himself."[25]

Because God is love, Moltmann declares, God suffers in solidarity with the poor and abandoned. Thus "a theology of the crucified God is the necessary foundation for a theology of liberation."[26] Liberation theologian Jon Sobrino agrees: "On the cross of Jesus, God himself is crucified. The Father suffers the death of the Son and takes upon himself all the pain and suffering of history. Thus, Christian existence is nothing else but . . . participating in this same process whereby God loves the world."[27]

With varying nuances, many feminist theologians also embrace the image of a God who suffers.[28] Of these, Elizabeth Johnson speaks with both the most boldness and the most caution. Having enumerated a catalog of historic brutalities, Johnson concludes:

> A God who is not in some way affected by such pain is not really worthy of human love and praise. A God who is simply a spectator of all this suffering, who can "permit" it, falls short of the modicum of decency expected at the human level. Such a God is morally intolerable.[29]

Johnson then demonstrates that a God incapable of tears is a construct of the male imagination, a deity burdened with macho values.

In the feminist value system, relationality, not power, is the supreme virtue.[30] For feminists, the vulnerability inherent in relationship is not necessarily an expression of weakness, but of love, freely given and overflowing in compassion.[31] "Speaking of the suffering of God from a feminist liberation perspective entails reshaping the notion of omnipotence . . . power not to prevent suffering but to transform it."[32] With the critical balance so characteristic of all her work, however, Johnson warns women in particular and theologians in general against glorifying suffering. "Anyone who works out a rational way to integrate evil and radical suffering . . . into a total intellectual system of which God is a part thereby justifies it. Such an effort, in my judgment, is doomed to fail."[33] The suggestions in this chapter are intended, not to justify suffering, but, where possible, to redeem it from meaninglessness.

The Eye of the Blackbird: Glimpsing God's Suffering

Swiftly moving, the eye of the blackbird sees sharply, but only in glimpses. Moreover, to use a pun, the individual "I," focused on the ego, actually blocks a vision of the whole. In no situation is this more evident—and disastrous—than when the "I" is in pain. Christians are accustomed to reminding themselves, usually when the worst is over, that "the sufferings of this present time are not worth comparing with the glory about to be revealed to us" (Rom 8:18). Even then, however, the thought is usually self-referential. But what if the "big picture" included divine suffering? While acknowledging that in the final analysis divine suffering remains a mystery, theologians have offered some creative explanations for it.[34]

God has chosen to act in this world, not through miraculous intervention, but through the two divine gifts in which, above all, humanity reflects God's image: creativity and freedom. God's suffering originates in that initial kenosis in which, without ceasing to be God, divine power voluntarily emptied itself into the cosmos, becoming vulnerable and defenseless, as source and model of unconditional love. From the beginning, therefore, God's suffering is inseparable from God's freedom—and ours. All creation, as well as humanity, is most "in the image of God" when it is free to be itself.[35] Contrary to the popular adage, God is not in the details; God is in the possibilities.[36] And, of course, those possibilities include the risk that freedom will be abused in the performance of evil. In an event of human violence, like the mass murders of 9/11/01 in New York City, God suffers with the victims and their survivors. But beyond that, God, even more than we, suffers from the perpetrators' abuse of the divine gift of freedom. In such situations God's "only hope" lies in the transformative response of other free human beings.

In the incarnation of Jesus, the divine kenosis invisible at the heart of creation becomes visible (Phil 2:5-6). "He who sees me sees the Father" (John 8:14). Moreover, the death and resurrection of Jesus, the source of life and hope for all creation, make visible, as symbol and reality, that pattern of death and resurrection found in all dimensions of an emerging universe.[37] In the supreme expression of love on the cross, Jesus takes kenosis a step further, choosing to experience the ultimate emptiness, divine abandonment: "My God, my God, why have you forsaken me?" (Mark 15:37; Ps 22:2).

According to Jon Sobrino, we can know intimacy with God by suffering with Jesus through the members of his Body, but Jesus' supreme suffering—separation from the Father—is not something we can choose for ourselves. "The closest we can get is to be profoundly present to those for whom God has chosen it."[38] And God is still present to those who can feel nothing but the divine absence. The Father did not order or condone the crucifixion; the crucifixion was ordered by human politicians who feared Jesus' power. Whenever human weakness, greed, or evil inflicts pain on humanity or on the earth, God suffers. When people "save" people from other people by killing them or when voracious human acquisition ravages landscapes, we hear again the voice of God's pain as he addresses Cain: "Listen; your brother's blood is crying out to me from the ground!" (Gen 4:10).

Inflections and Innuendoes: Sharing God's Suffering
A Lenten Experience

For most practicing Christians, Lent is a time to take on an exercise, or a program of exercises, intended to deepen our spiritual participation in the passion and death of Jesus. These rituals usually involve reading Scripture and making some tangible sacrifice of time, pleasure, or resources to benefit others. Here I would like to suggest a series of exercises inspired by the image of God presented above. They will probably take a little more thought than conventional Lenten practices and will probably demand less routine and physical discipline than sticking to a diet and a fitness program, but if successful, these reflections and practices will alter attitudes and behavior throughout the rest of the year.

❖ Make it your Lenten goal to put on the mind, the heart, the values of God by reflecting on the divine choice at the heart of creation.

> Let this same mind be in you
> that was in Christ Jesus,
>   who, though he was in the form of God,
>   did not regard equality with God
>   as something to be exploited,
> but emptied himself . . .
> and became obedient to the point of death
>   even death on a cross (Phil 2:5-8).

Try, then, to "empty" from your life one thing each day, beginning with things and proceeding to attitudes, compulsions, and emotions.

❖ Devote a few minutes a day to this consciousness-raising exercise. Reflect on the world around you, animate and inanimate, from the inside out. From this sacred inwardness, "Deep calleth unto deep." Listen to land, water, wildlife, trash heaps with an ear attuned to their *suffering*.

> exposing that inwardness will
> increase your pain, for you
> are part of this world.[39]

Meditate on how God's precarious love risks everything. Recall times when risking all for love has made your life richer/poorer. Set aside one day a week on which you deliberately live precariously, that is, in complete openness to whatever demands strangers may make on your time, your love, your trust. Record the outcomes of this experiment.

❖ Commenting on Mary's role in redemption, Teilhard de Chardin uses the term "passive action," that is, the action that functions simply by the transmission through us of divine energy.[40] Consider this statement in relation to any person you know who is incapable of action, and imagine that person as a source of divine energy. Think of an opportunity in which your own "passive action" might redeem a situation.

❖ According to current theological thought, evolution renders the traditional myth of the fall from a state of original perfection implausible. We are not struggling to recover an original perfection; rather, we are part of a struggle toward an ultimate fulfillment beyond our limited time in the process. For the Christian evolutionist, the good news is: "The age of expiation is over and done with once and for all."[41] So, God has forgiven everything—have you? Spend some time today canceling all emotional debts owed by you and to you. Then do something to celebrate your freedom.

❖ True knowledge of God is not natural, but "connatural." Connatural knowledge is the knowledge people have through sharing life and sharing pain. By suffering with Jesus in and through others, we gain a knowledge of God deeper than theology, deeper even than prayer.

❖ Global suffering is often the result of a Darwinian ethic: only the powerful deserve to survive. Ask yourself to what extent you endorse this thinking. Have you ever tried to persuade the powerful to explore alternatives for responding to violence without violence? How would a creative determination to minimize suffering ultimately redefine power? Could a redefinition of power eliminate war as a response to suffering? Are we comfortable with a lifestyle that demands the suffering of others?

❖ Someone has said, "We pray the prayer of supplication, not by words, but by acts." Compose a Litany of Divine Suffering that consists of headlines from your daily paper followed by the response: "Creator, Christ, and Spirit, draw compassion from us."[42] Recite your litany every day until you have done something to answer your own prayer.

❖ Not everyone can worship a vulnerable God who seems at the mercy of all the natural forces and unnatural exploitations to which an exquisitely beautiful universe is exposed. "Meditating on this notion will not make us happy. It will not increase our faith. It might increase our responsibility."[43]

Possibly only one of the suggestions above will appeal to you. If you think and do one thing differently for the rest of your life, this book will have achieved its purpose.

The following poem begins with a sense of worship inspired by the divine "emptying" and concludes with a heightened sense of human responsibility.

Kenosis

Where were you, God,
    before time began?

Were you thinking future,
    dreaming of what could be?

Or did you Three simply love
each other so much that your agape energy
    became the fireball
        that set in motion
            the evolution of matter and energy
                in our ever-expanding universe?
Did you empty yourselves so completely
that your creative imagination
spilled over in hydrogen and helium
        amoebas and anemones
    in moon, sun and stars
      jaw fish and octopi
    dinosaurs and dolphins
        penguins and pelicans
          herons and hawks
        radishes and rutabaga
          hollyhocks and hydrangea
    and all our kin
        and people of every shade and hue,
          of every temperament?

Are you still delighting in all you have wrought
    through a Word spoken in love?

How much more will you put up with
    before we completely devastate
        your magnificent work?

Do you ever wish time hadn't begun?

                        Mary McGuinness, O.P.

In the divine economy suffering is never wasted. As Teilhard de Chardin explains, "By the doctrine of the cross, we believe that the vast movement of agitation of human life opens onto a road which leads somewhere and that road climbs upward."[44] In his life and thought, Teilhard embodies a synthesis of scientific exploration with mystical experience that most of us experience only in brief flashes, usually when we are united with nature. Occasionally a film or a museum exhibit can put us in spiritual contact with the whole universe in its struggle toward fulfillment. This poem, inspired by a visit to the American Museum of Natural History, which included the Einstein Exhibit and the film *Kilimanjaro*, records such an event. Like mountain climbing, embracing science as sacred metaphor can be simultaneously a challenge to faith and an affirmation of it.

Kilimanjaro

High above the buried equator
   hacking through jungles
      clawing at rocks
         vaulting ravines
            sweating and freezing
               we inch our way
                  up, up into the thin
                      unbreathable air.
Far below, lesser snow peaks melt.
Tears cascading swiftly down
   subside to restful waters
      and irrigate valleys of
         food and flowers and
           fresh, green thirst.

            But not Mount Kilimanjaro:
              faceless mirror
                blinding
                sheer
                unyielding
                cold.

"After the first death," so many others:
dark nights, divorces, stillbirths, illusions
scattered like bones on the jagged slope
stone over stone over stone until
> *sublimation*
> from ice to air terminates
> in one *event horizon*
> from which the frozen heart
> knows no way down.

But here in the crystal silence
I hear a better poet declare:
"Death is the mother of beauty."[45]
> Far from the last camp fire
> burning snows ignite a final flare
> while before this glacial altar I
> repeat those words as a prayer.[46]

Elizabeth Michael Boyle, O.P.

In the end, for poets, as for everyone else, what happens on the mountaintop matters little; it's what we do about it when we come down that counts. Rainer Maria Rilke, to whom was granted many experiences of God's sublimity, also befriended God's poverty and suffering. It is not until the last line here that we recognize fully how the poet uses each familiar trope as a shocking metaphor to show our fastidious aversion to pain pushing God to the margins of our lives.

You are the poor one, you the destitute.
You are the stone that has no resting place.
You are the diseased one
whom we fear to touch.
Only the wind is yours.

You are poor like the spring rain
that gently caresses the city;
like wishes muttered in a prison cell, without a world to hold them.
And like the invalid, turning in his bed to ease the pain,
like flowers along the tracks, shuddering
as the train roars by, and like the hand
that covers our face when we cry—*that poor.*

Yours is the suffering of birds on a freezing night,
of dogs who go hungry for days.
Yours the long, sad waiting of animals
who are locked up and forgotten.

You are the beggar who averts his face,
the homeless person who has given up asking;
you howl in the storm.[47]

Rainer Maria Rilke

NOTES

[1] Makida, the Queen of Sheba, *Women in Praise of the Sacred: 43 Centuries of Spiritual Poetry by Women,* ed. Jane Hirshfield (New York: HarperCollins, 1994) 14.

[2] Christian de Duve, *Vital Dust* (New York: Basic Books, 1995) 9.

[3] Matthew Fox, *Meditations with Meister Eckhart: A Centering Book* (Santa Fe: Bear and Co., 1983), Meditation 92.

[4] Donald Nicholl, *Holiness* (Mahwah, NJ: Paulist Press, 1987) 20.

[5] Antoine Laurent Lavoisier, *Elements of Chemistry* (Philadelphia: Printed for Mathew Carey, Dec. 12, 1799). Epigraph to Jane Hirshfield, "The Wedding," *October Palace* (New York: HarperCollins, 1999).

[6] Pierre Teilhard de Chardin, *Hymn of the Universe* (London: Collins Fontana, 1970).

[7] Jon Sobrino, *Christology at the Crossroads: A Latin American Approach,* trans. John Drury (Maryknoll, NY: Orbis Books, 1978) 220.

[8] Ronald Goetz, "The Rise of a New Orthodoxy," in *Christian Century* (16 April 1986) 385–389.

[9] Richard Dawkins, *River Out of Eden* (New York: Basic Books, 1995) 131.

[10] Rainer Maria Rilke, "Wir dürfen dich nicht eigenmächtig malen," in *Rilke's Book of Hours: Love Poems to God,* trans. Anita Barrows and Joanna Macy (New York: Riverhead Books, 1997).

[11] Alfred North Whitehead, *Process and Reality: An Essay in Cosmology* (New York: Macmillan, 1960) 351.

[12] John Haught, *God after Darwin: A Theology of Evolution* (Boulder, CO: Westview Press, 2000) ch. 4.

[13] John Paul II, "Lord and Giver of Life" (Washington, DC: United States Catholic Conference, 1986) no. 39.

[14] Abraham Heschel, *The Prophets: An Introduction* (New York: Harper Colophon Books, 1955). Thomas G. Weinandy, O.F.M., who identifies Heschel as an

important influence, devotes a whole chapter to refuting his arguments: *Does God Suffer?* (South Bend: University of Notre Dame Press, 2000) 8, 64–68.

[15] Heschel, *The Prophets*, 224–225. For a more recent exposition of Old Testament evidence, see T. E. Freitheim, *The Suffering of God: An Old Testament Perspective* (Philadelphia: Fortress Press, 1984).

[16] Heschel, *The Prophets*, 271. Heschel never ignores Tillich's caveat: "A religious symbol is idolatrous unless it suggests its own inadequacy." See Introduction, n. 17.

[17] Ibid., 218–219.

[18] Ibid., 48.

[19] The "process theology" movement, begun by Protestant scholars in the 1930s, did not take hold among Catholics until the sixties.

[20] Diarmuid O'Murchu, *Evolutionary Faith: Rediscovering God in Our Great Story* (Maryknoll, NY: Orbis Books, 2003) 79.

[21] John Robert Baker, "The Christological Symbol of God's Suffering," in *Religious Experience and Process Theology: The Pastoral Implications of a Major Modern Movement,* ed. Harry James Cargas and Bernard Lee (New York: Paulist Press, 1976) 99.

[22] Haught, *God after Darwin*, 45.

[23] Archibald MacLeish, *J.B.: A Play in Verse* (New York: Houghton Mifflin, 1986) 11.

[24] Elie Wiesel, *Night* (London: Collins, 1972) 76–77.

[25] Jürgen Moltmann, *The Crucified God: The Cross of Christ as the Foundation and Criticism of Christian Theology* (New York: Harper and Row, 1974) 277–278.

[26] Ibid., 227.

[27] Sobrino, *Christology at the Crossroads*, 224.

[28] Dorothee Soelle, 1975; Rosemary Haughton, 1981; Monica Hellwig, 1983; Grace Jantzen, 1984; Elizabeth Johnson, 1993.

[29] Elizabeth A. Johnson, C.S.J., *She Who Is: The Mystery of God in Feminist Theological Discourse* (New York: Crossroad, 1993) 249.

[30] Ibid., 252–253. The influence of feminist theology's critique of power is evident in John Haught's argument that Intelligent Design Theory reflects a preference for power that is not compatible with the Christian concept of the divine kenosis involved in Incarnation. Haught, *God after Darwin*, 48.

[31] Johnson, *She Who Is,* 65.

[32] Ibid., 269.

[33] Ibid., 271.

[34] Notably, Rahner, Schillebeecx, Moltmann, and Haught.

[35] Haught, *God after Darwin*, 39.

[36] Baker, "The Christological Symbol," 99.

[37] Here the symbolism expressed by Cletus Wessels is really reciprocal: nature prefigures the paschal mystery of which Jesus is both symbol and reality. *Jesus in the New Universe Story* (Maryknoll, NY: Orbis Books, 2003) 219.

[38] Sobrino, *Christology at the Crossroads*, 223.

[39] Robert Penn Warren, "Riddle in the Garden," in *Incarnations* (New York: Random House, 1968).

[40] Teilhard de Chardin, letter to Marguerite, cited in Ursula King, *The Life and Vision of Teilhard de Chardin* (Maryknoll, NY: Orbis Books, 1996) 11.

[41] Haught, *God after Darwin,* 141.

[42] *Hildegard of Bingen's Book of Divine Works with Letters and Songs,* ed. and trans., Matthew Fox (Santa Fe: Bear and Co., 1987) 366.

[43] O'Murchu, *Evolutionary Faith,* 79.

[44] Teilhard de Chardin, *The Divine Mileu: An Essay on the Interior Life* (New York: Harper and Brothers, 1960) 77.

[45] Dylan Thomas: "After the first death, there is no other." Wallace Stevens: "Death is the mother of Beauty."

[46] *Sublimation:* the unique process by which glaciers at the highest altitudes transform into air without melting; *event horizon:* Einstein's term for "point of no return."

[47] Rainer Maria Rilke, "Du bist der Arme, du der Mittellose," in *Rilke's Book of Hours: Love Poems to God,* trans. Anita Barrows and Joanna Macy (New York: Riverhead Books, 1996).

Chapter Five

REFLECTIONS ON EVOLVING CONSCIOUSNESS

"Day to day pours forth speech,
and night to night declares knowledge.
There is no speech, nor are there words;
their voice is not heard;
Yet their voice goes out through all the earth,
and their words to the end of the world."
(Psalm 19:2-4)

God to Abraham: "If it weren't for me, you wouldn't be here."
Abraham to God: "True, but if it weren't for me,
there wouldn't be anyone to think about you."
(Jewish Folk Tale)[1]

"The world is presence and not force.
Presence is not mind.
It fills the being before the mind can think."
(Wallace Stevens)[2]

"Christ is present even in subatomic particles—
energizing the process
towards its goal of higher consciousness."
(Pierre Teilhard de Chardin, S.J.)[3]

"One of the great satisfactions of the human spirit
is to feel that one's family extends
across the borders of the species to everything that lives."
(Stanley Kunitz)[4]

"The work of a rock is to ponder whatever is,
an act that looks singly like prayer
but is not prayer.

What difference does it make whether
the rock prays or not
if it leads me into prayer?"
(Jane Hirshfield)[5]

In the light of evolutionary science, consciousness, like everything else, must be redefined as an ongoing event or a process. When microbiologist Lynn Margulis and physicist Dana Zohar characterize evolution as "a series of creative unions in a progression toward higher degrees of consciousness and unity,"[6] it seems logical to ask "consciousness of and unity with *what*?" Neither scientist answers that question. Yet their language, "progression toward higher degrees of consciousness and unity," sounds analogous to the parallel degrees of knowledge and love that mystics say accompany the journey to union with God. What science calls "higher consciousness," process theology calls "the goal of the world, God's self-communication to all the spiritual subjectivities of the cosmos."[7]

Before we scale the cliffs of "higher consciousness," however, perhaps we need to ask ground-level questions like: What exactly do we mean by consciousness? How does it manifest itself? Are human beings alone endowed with consciousness? What difference does it make? How do these questions relate to everyday spirituality? Our task in this chapter is not to hone precise definitions and distinctions, but to select from among volumes of fascinating speculation sufficient understanding to inspire faith and praxis.

A Way of Looking: Consciousness in the Evolutionary Process

Even among scientifically educated adults who know that there is no such thing as inanimate matter, that even stones are alive with quantum energy, not all are aware that science is moving relentlessly closer to the concept that an indefinable consciousness impels this inner force. Virtually all contemporary scientists who have addressed the subject detect some level of consciousness, not only in humanity and other animal species but in everything in the universe, both subatomic particles and planets.

The notion that plants, animals, and even rocks are endowed with some form of awareness or sensitivity, an idea that predates Socrates, is known to philosophers as *panpsychism*. Today variations of panpsychism are being seriously reconsidered by scientists. David Bohm, for example, suggests a level of primitive protoconsciousness even at the level of subatomic particles.[8] At the high end of the continuum from the invisible to the visible, from simple to complex organisms, animals exhibit varying degrees of awareness and intention, and science now questions the assumption that humanity alone seems endowed with self-consciousness and freedom.

Moreover, self consciousness is not regarded by all philosophers as a blessing. In fact, in what came to be named "The Romantic Myth," philosophers identified self-consciousness as the equivalent of original sin, that is, the fall-out of *identity* with nature into the subject-object relationship. Now some psychologists and philosophers assert that human consciousness creates reality.[9] Perhaps no one has expressed faith in the power of subjective consciousness more confidently than the poet Rilke:

I know that nothing has ever been real
without my beholding it.
All becoming has needed me.
My looking ripens things
and they come toward me,
to meet and be met.[10]

Rainer Maria Rilke

In relation to human consciousness, Teilhard de Chardin's version of evolution is particularly interesting. Teilhard believed that biological evolution is essentially finished, but the process is now advancing beyond the biosphere into what he calls the *"noosphere,"* that is, from human self-consciousness outward into a network of conscious minds expressed in cultures, politics, science, and the technologies that link them.[11] Without realizing it, perhaps, Teilhard suggests the path of "salvation" from the original sin of subjectivity.

Clearly, no single definition carries a denotation sufficiently protean to encompass all these varieties and manifestations of "consciousness," but scientists and psychologists continue to be fascinated by the challenge. In their attempts, some scientists, while dutifully denouncing all matter/spirit dualism, are forced to use dualistic language to specify what consciousness is *not*. "We should not be surprised," says David Hoffman, "that despite centuries of effort by the most brilliant minds, there is as yet no *physicalist* theory of consciousness, no theory that explains how mindless matter or energy or field could be or cause, conscious experience."[12] Dana Zohar, in her study subtitled "Consciousness Defined by the New Physics," also insists: "Consciousness cannot be reduced to the activities of vibrating molecules. We are not our brains."[13]

Increasingly, however, some scientists are using *consciousness* to designate "the activity of either a transcendent or immanent agency, working to create or shape the material world from the beginning of time."[14] Zohar herself disdains such terminology as "bordering on traditional mysticism or theology,"[15] as indeed it does. However, the scientific vocabulary she immediately substitutes raises language to an even more exasperating degree of mystical obscurity. Consciousness, Zohar explains, evolves out of a "creative dialogue between a quantum coherence and neural tissue," both dependent on "relationship to a pre-existing, all-embracing ground-state of consciousness."[16] Zohar's definition illustrates the linguistic contortions to which secularists are driven to maintain a sturdy wall between science and religion, at the same time insisting that all reality is one.

As we grope through the miasma of Zohar's daunting definition, we can cling to one familiar word—"relationship." Consciousness, even self-consciousness, always involves relationship. Dynamic relationship is a condition of life—or death. The human person itself emerges out of a process that moves from self-preservation to self-adaptation to self-transcendence.[17] The magnet for this self-transcendence is the universal "yearning" toward something more than the self. "Every creation of matter . . . is a recapitulation of all past creation and carries an inherent propensity to become something more than it is at any present moment."[18] Modern micro-technology now enables us to observe analogous processes of preservation, adaptation, and transcendence being acted out in miniature at the quantum level.[19] Even in micro-organisms, scientists detect both a "tendency toward inwardness" in one direction and an attraction toward "symbiotic" relationships in the other. Technology has simply confirmed what Whitehead and Teilhard intuited as a "within-ness" in matter, accelerating as it advances from atoms to human beings. At the same time, in all creatures, the huge and the microscopic, there appears a discernible drive outward in what philosopher Hans Jonas calls "a cosmogonic eros."[20] The tension between these two drives engenders the consciousness "event."

Those who find these explanations of scientists and philosophers exhausting may find one mother's reflection on the evolution of consciousness more appealing:

First Thought

Did it appear
like the tracks
of the red fox in snow
or did it flare first
in a burst of star dust
when the earth was dark
and knew nothing of chestnuts
or design

only the promise
seeded into the void
where Eden and Atlantis
and the horse fly's green eyes
and all that matters
lay in the percolating potential
aglow with a future
still to flower.

Was it strained through the sieve
of some primordial wind
in the sub atomic well-spring
firing spinning oscillating
the way oxygen and hydrogen
danced around each other
in the cosmic chaos
becoming the mother of water.

Fragile globe of the infant's head
sacristy of imagination
housing bundles of neurons
firing spinning oscillating
dancing in the sub atomic well spring
coming
coming
becoming.

Marion Goldstein

At a point in the history of human consciousness after language and before sophisticated social structures, Bede Griffiths places the development of symbolic imagination simultaneously with the beginnings of spirituality.[21] Poetry like that of Gerard Manley Hopkins in Chapter One (see p. 6) seems to recapitulate the moment, capturing in symbolic imagery both exciting and accessible the subjective interiority of things and their desire to express it in their unique languages. For those who prefer a visual vocabulary, Vincent Van Gogh's pulsating canvases demonstrate how an artist's sensitivity to other-than-human consciousness compelled him to translate the vibrant interior life of stars, cypresses, and wheat fields into color and movement.

Can human consciousness interact with other-than-human inhabitants of our planet, and does it matter? Scientific experiments have actually demonstrated that human consciousness can have an "emotional" impact on "inanimate" matter. Among the most celebrated examples would be that by a Japanese artist who photographed molecules of pure water as they responded positively to the blessing of a Buddhist monk and to words like "Thank you" and "Love." He then photographed these same molecules as they reacted negatively to "You make me sick."[22] At Duke University's Center for Spirituality, Theology, and Health and at other research venues, the hypothesis that states of consciousness can influence matter motivates research testing the possible effect of belief and prayer on health and healing. Anecdotal evidence from such studies regularly makes news from Los Angeles to New York. As one article reports, however, from the first probings by Darwin's student in 1860 to the present, inconclusive findings seem to reflect the bias of the researchers.[23]

Though few people habitually engage in conversation with quarks and quanta, most of us have experienced a sense of consciousness at least among some of our biological brothers and sisters. As far back as Virgil's untranslatable "tears in things," poets, in particular, seem to specialize in non-verbal, inter-species dialogue, as the following citations will illustrate.

> There's something very important to me about having a kind
> of relationship with plants and animals, that can be transacted
> wholly without language. . . . I have a tendency when I'm walking
> in the garden, to brush the flowers as I go by, anticipating the
> fragrant eloquence of their response. I get a sense of *reciprocity*
> that is very comforting, very consoling.[24]

I am one of those who has no trouble imagining the sentient lives of
trees, of their leaves in some fashion communicating . . . or . . . knowing it is I who have come.[25]

"I believe everything has a soul."
Who has it, and who doesn't?
Why should I and not
        the camel, the anteater,
        the trees, the stones, roses,
            lemons, grass
            blue iris.[26]

I was barely
old enough to ask and repeat its name.
    . . .
It looked at me, I looked
back, delight
filled me as if
I, not the flower,
were a flower and were brimful of rain.
    . . .
Perhaps through a lifetime what I've desired
has always been to return
to that endless giving and receiving
of that attention
that once-in-a-lifetime
secret communion.[27]

Some scientists no longer dismiss such sentiments as "mere whimsy."
They recognize that "communion with other species," practiced by
the human community at large, could have profound practical consequences. Would advocacy for endangered species fall upon so many
deaf ears if more of us enjoyed "interpersonal relationships" with trees
and wild animals similar to those we enjoy with our pets? Cosmologist
Brian Swimme urges us to a profound conversion of consciousness,
which he calls "comprehensive compassion."[28] He points out that even
philanthropic endeavors tend to limit the concept of compassion to the
human sphere, whereas a scientific worldview encompasses all of creation in its concern. Although the name of Darwin was at first associated
more with brutality than with compassion, the dynamics of Darwinian
biology favor the cultivation of each animal's capacity for caring and

bonding. This genetic mutation introduced among mammals some 220 million years ago endowed them and eventually us with a higher chance of survival. In reaching this conclusion, neo-Darwinians are once again "catching up" with the vision of all the wisdom traditions. Ancient mystics, sages, and shamans on all continents teach that transcending self-centeredness carries the psyche beyond itself into fulfillment in others and in the Other.

Humans are the first species with the imaginative capacity to care about all species. Yet, in recent decades human consumption has been responsible for an alarming acceleration of species extinction. Human environmental impact has raised the rate of extinction among other-than-human species from one extinction every five years to twenty-five thousand species per year. Swimme believes that the only way to rein in such decimation "would be to reinvent ourselves at the species level in a way that enables us to live in mutually enhancing relationships . . . not only with humans but with all beings."[29] Such a global Utopia requires a radical shift in priorities from the human individual to the earth community, from an economy of consumption and accumulation to one of preservation. Perhaps only a global catastrophe could provoke the kind of metanoia Swimme requires.

Meanwhile, like evolution itself, a series of small permutations in consciousness is paving the way. For a quarter-century study groups and retreats have been including ecosensitivity training sessions that have broadened the scope of spirituality. Recently the reappearance of one ivory-billed woodpecker, long presumed extinct, had a remarkable effect on the personal morale of one such group, which adopted the bird as a metaphor for hope. At a time when physical and moral violence seems targeted at children and human decency itself seems "endangered," the event illustrated for me how the weakest among us can bring a gift of strength and unity to the earth community.

Survivor

Here on the brink of
ultimate midnight
a single black egg
shivers in its black nest.

One small ivory blade
taps at the shell
opens a jagged crack
and tastes the cool air.

Struggling through
        the broken wall
                limp feathers startle
                        the icy dew.

Blind instinct drills
        a hole in extinction
                and fragile wings
                        lift a dying planet
                                into the light.

Elizabeth Michael Boyle, O.P.

Even from a strictly human perspective, great potential for peace could accrue within the world community from the "consciousness-raising" activity of treating plants, animals, and minerals as having "personalities," as having a future, as having "been endowed by their creator" with inalienable rights. Surely such possibilities are among the meanings Jane Hirshfield intended when she chose the allusive title for her poem "The Kingdom." Simply reading it evokes a hunger for Isaiah's "peaceable kingdom," where lions, lambs, and children lie down together in "homeland security" (Isa 11:6).

From *The Kingdom*

At times
the heart
stands back
and looks at the mind,
as a lion
quietly looks
at the not-quite itself,
not-quite-another,
moving of shadows and grass.
. . .

Then seeing
all that will be
heart once again enters—
enters hunger, enters sorrow;
enters finally losing it all.
To know if nothing else,
what it once owned.[30]

Jane Hirshfield

In our global village, where so many educated citizens are hopelessly monolingual, developing sensitivity to non-verbal expression among all inhabitants of our planet could go a long way toward easing transcultural communication. The most eloquent non-verbal communication we can learn from plants and animals is listening.

The Eye of the Blackbird: Seeing and Being Seen by God

The eye of evolutionary science sees all things moving from instinct toward consciousness; the eye of faith sees all things moving from mystery to revelation toward deeper mystery. In the innate, universal drive toward unity in higher consciousness that scientists detect even in entities we used to consider "inanimate," we can find a metaphor for the sacred truth intuited by St. Paul: "Creation waits with eager longing for the revealing of the children of God" (Rom 8:20). This "eager longing" unites all creation in a chorus echoing the often-quoted words of Augustine: "Lord, our hearts are restless until they rest in you."[31] Moreover, now that science has led us to appreciate the "within-ness" of God, we remind ourselves that we do not *move toward* God at all, just toward a greater *consciousness* of the incredible fact that we are there, in God, already. For the scientifically aware, the psalmist's familiar words assume a joyous tone:

Where can I go from your spirit?
    Or where can I flee from your presence?
If I ascend to heaven, you are there,
    if I make my bed in Sheol, you are there (Ps 139:7-8).

We are not so much under God's scrutiny as *within* God's consciousness. And to be within God's consciousness means, not to dissolve into some kind of mystic oblivion, but to incarnate God's attitude toward the world around us by a more intense awareness of it. In fact, awareness of the world—grateful, critical, and compassionate—might be considered a barometer of our progress toward *deeper* consciousness within our creator.

From the beginning of the universe, the creator's attitude toward the world has been characterized by incredible—some might say irresponsible—trust. Pathways of both the Old and New Testaments are paved with parables that dramatize human trust in God, but seldom do we recognize a parable that reverses the positions. At last, modern science has given us one: at the instant of the Big Bang, God launches the barque of the universe onto a turbulent sea of possibility in an act of perfect trust. Matthew's narrative of Jesus asleep in the apostles' boat repeats that parable (Matt 8:23-27), and the apostles' reprimand mimics history's cry: "Why do you sleep, O Lord?" (Ps 44:23). Slumbering in a fragile, storm-tossed craft, Jesus presents a striking image of God's perfect trust in nature and in the fishermen who, for better or worse, are *in charge*. Human trust equivalent to Jesus' trust in the apostles would launch a miracle far more useful than taming the Sea of Galilee. At the moment I can think of no international crisis that could not be averted or alleviated if human beings trusted one another as the Creator has trusted us.

Re-reading the Gospels with an evolutionary view of revelation helps us to understand that God's self-communication in Scripture does not comprise the "whole truth." For each succeeding generation God's self-communication is modulated by new knowledge and new faith experiences. It is possible to read the Gospel story titled "The Finding of the Child Jesus in the Midst of the Doctors" (Luke 2:41-52) as a parable about human consciousness in relation to revelation itself. In this interpretation, Mary and Joseph in search of their lost child represent the search of God's people for a way of understanding that has been lost—and their finding of a new and better one. What Jesus reveals to the doctors is addressed to *humanity's level of understanding at that point in time.* Everything humanity understood about God before Jesus is analogous to what could be explained to adults by a twelve-year-old child. In fact, human understanding, especially in relation to God, always needs to mature. Evolutionary thinking, as well as the role of the Spirit in the believing community, encourages us to believe that there is always more, not less, to each Gospel story. Luke's episode concludes with Jesus returning to eighteen more years of patient preparation for his revelatory mission. Modern biblical scholarship has exhaustively debated the issue of Jesus' level of self-awareness at this age. Regardless of the status of that debate, Jesus' lengthy maturation symbolically urges humanity to patient humility in its quest for a consciousness of God that is still maturing.

The Incarnation was a mode of revelation that profoundly facilitated both our consciousness of God and our relationship to a sacred universe. I suggest that the modern tendency to depersonalize language about God does not necessarily advance the agenda either of revelation or of ecospirituality. I mention this because during the study that accompanied writing this book, I observed an ironic paradox. At precisely the time when many theologians are using science to dismantle the concept of a personal God, scientists are urging us to cultivate a "personal relationship" with everything else. With relief, I turned to Karl Rahner, a theologian who consistently respects science, prayer, and human history as sources of revelation. Acknowledging that the word "person" applies to God by way of analogy, Rahner asserts:

> If anything at all can be predicated of God, then the concept of "personhood" has to be predicated . . . only if we allow God to be a person in the way in which he in fact wants to encounter us and has encountered us in our individual histories, in the depths of our consciousness, and in the whole history of the human race.[32]

Rahner rejects as contrary to reason

> the notion that the absolute ground of all reality is something like an unconscious and impersonal cosmic law . . . a source which empties itself out without possessing itself, which gives rise to spirit and freedom without itself being spirit and freedom, the notion of a blind, primordial ground of the world which cannot look at us even if it wants to . . . .[33]

In the profound depths of prayer, Rahner continues, the human person "experiences itself as having its origins in another and as being given to itself from another . . . ."[34] Such personalism seems to me to foster the sense of mutuality with the earth and the universe that ecologists strive to instill.

To embrace both science and a personal God as multivalent metaphors for the same reality weakens neither God nor science. On the contrary, personalism roots our relationship to both God and the natural world in the responsible love and choice that distinguish human consciousness from all coolly detached "cosmic subjectivities." Ecofeminist Sallie McFague concurs that the reduction of the personal God to hidden creativity or unpredictable grace is neither desirable nor necessary.[35] Imaging God as Father, Mother, Beloved, and Friend avoids both the impersonality of praying "to whom it may concern" and the futile "religious solipsism" of praying to "the God within ourselves."[36] More importantly, personal imagery demands more of us than stoic abstractions do. "It is impossible to conceive of love as simply *there . . .* alone. Love has to be given and received."[37]

Ideally, consciousness at the level of choice becomes *conscience*, for conscience involves accountability. Beatrice Bruteau envisions human consciousness in the present age as at the moment of "the Grand Option," when human choices will determine whether the universe goes forward into higher-level *unities* or falls back into entropy, that is, ultimate decomposition.[38] Only the image of God as *love* can elicit the kind of sustained reciprocal relationship with the natural universe demanded by "the Grand Option." Responsible human beings feel more accountable to a person than to an idea, however noble. Freedom infused with love goes beyond passive participation in a process to become co-creativity. The "higher-level unity" of a new science-based spirituality will neither negate nor submerge the most vital metaphors of the tradition. On the contrary, metaphors of a personal God will nourish the new soil as immigrant cultures flourish in the freedom of a new homeland.

Inflections and Innuendoes
A Resurrection/Post Resurrection Experience

Whether we read the Gospels of the Easter season as history or as symbolic parables, the truth at the center of the story chimes with incontestable scientific fact: all life is a resurrection from death. Christian understanding of Jesus' resurrection has been shaped largely by the New Testament. But, Scripture scholars remind us, for the first Christians this was not so. The first Christian community moved through an evolution of consciousness that began with the experience of God's presence in the Risen Jesus and eventually found written expression in the appearance narratives.[39] Christian experience of the Risen Jesus dictated the Scriptures, not the other way around. Among theologians, consciousness of the Resurrection is still evolving from interpretation of what happened, to celebration of what is still happening in individuals and in the world. Whatever the disciples understood, contemporary Christians, liberated from literalism, know more.[40]

We now understand resurrection as both a reality and a symbol of a transformation totally different from mere resuscitation of a crucified body. The way the Gospel authors render this difference is to characterize Jesus as physically unrecognizable. Interpreting the appearance narratives at the symbolic level, Cletus Wessels hails the resurrection of Jesus as "a qualitatively new moment, . . . a deeper level of human consciousness flowing from the chaos of the crucifixion . . . enabling the Jesus community to experience the meaning of death . . . as a re-entry into the consciousness of God."[41]

In his analysis of our own participation in the Resurrection, Wessel asserts: "When I die, I will return to Mother Earth and re-enter the Consciousness of the Earth out of which I emerged, and this consciousness is God."[42] Here the ecotheologian's eloquent enthusiasm seems to carry him into several contradictions. How can we "re-enter" a reality from which we have never been separated? And in a book titled *Jesus in the New Universe Story,* why restrict God's consciousness to a single planet? Might it not be more accurate to say: Resurrection liberates human consciousness from all bodily and intellectual limitations, so that we can enjoy full consciousness of life in God's unconditional love?

A number of theologians have pointed out that death and resurrection are simultaneous and that the dead, united to God, are wherever God is.[43] Our resurrection experience, therefore, extends beyond the Easter season to include consciousness of the presence of our beloved dead wherever God is—which is everywhere. Theologizing about the transformation of consciousness does not, however, satisfy curiosity about the resurrection of the body. We do not know what happened to the body of Jesus after he no longer needed it to convince his disciples that he was alive. Nor can we be sure what ultimately happens to our own bodies. I like Wessel's suggestion that the human individual survives as "flesh transformed into light."[44] The scientific image lets me see my beloved dead among the flaming tapers surrounding me at the Easter Vigil liturgy, in the endlessly multiplied, undivided radiance of unconditional love.

There are times when nature itself seems to set the stage for illumination. Sometimes even a natural annoyance can distract us into mystery.

The Fly

After tunneling in my hair
buzzingbuzzing
he lighted, a black blob
on the white cabinet.
I had a dish towel in my hand
and the thought of his demise
erupted naturally as water
from a spring.
It wouldn't take much effort
to slap him senseless with a swinging towel.

I had stalked before
when murderous intention crossed my mind
before a plan or weapon was devised
had watched a gossamer thing
lift its papery wings and fling
itself to the ceiling
but this one seemed to linger, preoccupied
on the deathbed of the door.

One swat—he fell onto the countertop
near a bowl of marinating mushrooms
tried to lift himself and fell again—
back shuddering, hocks clawing
he flopped.
I couldn't bear to watch
the opulence of death
and yet cessation of that buzzingbuzzing
was restorative and I could think again.

I swiped him off the counter
and ground his heart and blood and lungs
in the sink eradicator
and it was then
I knew
the God who made me
made him
and I wondered about all creatures
both winged and flawed

who sense impending doom from afar
aglow with a future yet to flower
knowing more than could be known
they soar.

Marion Goldstein

For me, darkness in nature usually heightens consciousness of interior light, and natural noises drive me into an inner cave of stillness. On one occasion this cave opened into a gloriously empty tomb.

Now and at the Hour

Outside
winds howl
trees flail
grey clouds darken
to black.

Inside
light chimes
above the printed page
gathers to a stillness
listens.

    "Those who die no longer have to wait for resurrection." [45]
No longer have:
    Let go all books
        all thought
            all wordless desire.
                Let go of letting go.
No longer wait.
    Death is life
        in a new translation
            whose syllables rename
                all loneliness.
No longer die:
    Let death reclaim your loveliness.

Elizabeth Michael Boyle, O.P.

NOTES

[1] Cited in Timothy Ferris, *The Whole Shebang* (New York: Simon and Shuster, 1997) 292.

[2] Wallace Stevens, "Saint John and the Black Hole," in *Collected Poetry and Prose* (New York: Library Classics of the United States, 1997).

[3] Teilhard de Chardin, cited by Ewert Cousins, "Process Models in Culture, Philosophy, and Theology," in *Process Theology: Basic Writings by Key Thinkers of a Major Modern Movement* (New York: Newman Press, 1971) 18.

[4] Stanley Kunitz, *The Wild Braid: A Poet Reflects on a Century in the Garden* (New York: W. W. Norton, 2005) 54.

[5] Jane Hirshfield, "Rock," in *Given Sugar, Given Salt* (New York: HarperCollins, 2001).

[6] Lynn Margulis, *The Symbiotic Planet: A New Look at Evolution* (New York: Basic Books, 1996); Dana Zohar, *The Quantum Self* (New York: William Morrow, 1990).

[7] Karl Rahner, "Christology within an Evolutionary View of the World," in *A Rahner Reader* (New York: Seabury Press, 1975) 166–167.

[8] David Bohm, "A New Theory of the Relationship of Mind and Matter," in *The Journal of the American Society of Psychical Research,* vol. 80, no.2 (1986) 129.

[9] Northrop Frye, "The Romantic Myth," in *A Study of English Romanticism* (New York: Random House, 1968) 17.

[10] Rainer Maria Rilke, "Da neigt sich die Stunde und ruhrt mich an," in *Rilke's Book of Hours: Love Poems to God,* trans. Anita Barrows and Joanna Macy (New York: Riverhead Books, 1997).

[11] Teilhard de Chardin, *The Human Phenomenon* (Portland, OR: Sussex Academic Press, 1999) 191–194.

[12] Hoffman is responding to the question posed to scientists, "What do you believe is true even though you cannot prove it?" "The *Edge* Annual Question—2005," Edge: The World Question Center. Online at http://www.edge.org. For a fuller discussion of the issue, see David Chalmers, *The Conscious Mind: In Search of a Fundamental Theory* (New York: Oxford, 1996).

[13] Zohar, *The Quantum Self,* 102.

[14] Ibid., 220.

[15] Ibid.

[16] Ibid., 221–222.

[17] Cletus Wessels, *Jesus in the New Universe Story* (Maryknoll, NY: Orbis Books, 2003) 58.

[18] Diarmuid O'Murchu, *Quantum Theology: Spiritual Implications of the New Physics* (New York: Crossroad, 2003) 57–58.

[19] Ibid.

[20] Hans Jonas, *Mortality and Morality* (Evanston, IL: Northwestern University Press, 1996) 170ff.

[21] Bede Griffiths, *A New Vision of Reality* (Springfield, IL: Templegate Publishers, 1983) 33–48.

[22] *What the Bleep Do We (K)now!?* A film by William Arntz, et al. Twentieth Century Fox Home Entertainment, 2004.

[23] Dyanash Jathr, "Can Prayer Heal: A Growing Number of Studies Look for Clues," http://www.theweekmagazine.com (31 July 2005).

[24] Kunitz, *The Wild Braid,* 53.

[25] Mary Oliver, *Winter Hours: Prose, Prose Poems and Poems* (Boston: Mariner Books, 2004) 15.

[26] Mary Oliver, *Blue Pastures* (New York: Harvest Books, 1995) 64; "Some Questions You Might Ask," in *New and Selected Poems* (Boston: Beacon Press, 1992).

[27] Denise Levertov, "First Love," in *The Great Unknowing: Last Poems* (New York: New Directions, 1999).

[28] Brian Swimme, "Comprehensive Compassion." Interview in *What Is Enlightenment Magazine* (Spring/Summer, 2001).

[29] Ibid.

[30] From Jane Hirshfield, "The Kingdom," in *The October Palace* (New York: Harper Perennial, 1994).

[31] *Confessions of St. Augustine,* trans. Frank Sheed (New York: Sheed and Ward, 1943) 1.

[32] Karl Rahner, *Foundations of Christian Faith: An Introduction to the Idea of Christianity,* trans. William V. Dych (New York: Crossroad, 1978) 74.

[33] Ibid., 75.

[34] Ibid.

[35] Sallie McFague, *Models of God: Theology for an Ecological, Nuclear Age* (Philadelphia: Fortress Press, 1987) 80. McFague refers specifically to Gordon Kaufman, *Theology for a Nuclear Age* (Philadelphia: Westminster Press, 1985). The title of his more recent work carries forward his agenda of theological depersonalization: *In the Beginning, Creativity* (Minneapolis: Fortress Press, 2004).

[36] Rabbi Abraham Heschel, *Man's Quest for God: Studies in Prayer and Symbolism* (New York: Charles Scribner's Sons, 1954) 56.

[37] Rosemary Haughton, *The Passionate God* (New York: Paulist Press, 1981) 21.

[38] Beatrice Bruteau, "A Song That Goes On Singing: An Interview by Amy Adelstein and Ellen Daly," *What Is Enlightenment Magazine* (Spring/Summer, 2002) 3.

[39] Wessels, *Jesus in the New Universe Story,* 129.

[40] Donald Goergen, cited by Wessels, 129.

[41] Ibid., 132.

[42] Ibid., 125.

[43] Karl Rahner, "The Life of the Dead," in *Theological Investigations* 4, trans. Kevin Smyth (Baltimore: Helicon, 1966).

[44] Ibid., 134.

[45] Ibid.

Chapter Six

REFLECTIONS ON STRING THEORY

"A distant, plucked, infinitesimal string
The obligation due to everything
That's smaller than the universe."
(Gjertrud Schnakenberg)[1]

"Nature is sustained by a superhuman,
pulsating restlessness, a type of resonance,
vibrating throughout time and eternity."
(Diarmuid O'Murchu)[2]

"God is the web, the energy, the space, the light
—not captured in them—. . .
but revealed in that singular, vast net of relationships
that animates everything that is."
(Barbara Brown Taylor)[3]

"When an individual dies,
the web connecting all life remains . . . reconstituted.
The whole construct is renewed;
the individual creatures who inhabit the web keep changing."
(Stanley Kunitz)[4]

"The greater the coherence is an infallible sign of the greater truth."
(Teilhard de Chardin)[5]

"Matter itself is profoundly social."
(Elizabeth Johnson)[6]

Pure theology, by nature of its invisible, untestable subject matter, always includes acts of imagination. Science, too, depends upon the power to imagine beyond what appears to the senses. This desideratum appears strikingly evident in the phenomenon known as *string theory*. At this moment, after forty years of speculation,[7] string theory exists nowhere outside the fertile imaginations of string theorists themselves.[8] Not one of the scientists who is currently devoting a life's work to string theory has ever actually seen a "string," though each has sketched thousands of imaginary ones. Because string theory is, at least at the present time, untestable, and because to date no experiment has been devised to prove that strings exist, some scientists have declared that it is not science at all, that it should be labeled either a new discipline or a philosophy.[9] Of course, such objections neither prove nor disprove that strings exist, only that they cannot be proved to exist. (Does something sound familiar?)

What's more, string theory demands faith in several unimaginable postulates: that there are not four dimensions but ten or eleven; that sedate Newtonian equations can place astronauts on the moon, while in a "parallel universe" unmanageable quarks gallop through "the Wild West of quantum mechanics,"[10] reversing the laws of gravity. Actually, it was the frustration of physics with such contradictions between the rules that seem to govern the macrocosm of stars and galaxies and the lawless behaviors that prevail in the microcosms of photons and neutrons that initially sparked the inquiry called string theory. In the experience of theoretical physicists, however, "things that seem incredibly different can really be manifestations of the same underlying phenomena."[11]

For almost a century the Grail Quest of modern physics has been the search for a Theory of Everything that would reconcile two apparently contradictory but demonstrably "true" pictures of reality. According to Brian Greene, author of the most popular expositions of the string theory, "the ultimate theory would provide an unshakable pillar of coherence forever assuring us that the universe is a comprehensible place."[12] While string theory is still in its infancy, and its mathematical complexities remain beyond the comprehension of non-specialists, there is plenty of room to speculate on its implications as sacred metaphor. Following the example of string theorists, let's imagine that what they imagine is true.

Looking with the Eye of Imagination

Mathematics, like myth, is an image contrived to deal with an abstraction, either to deduce a reality before it is discovered or to explain a real problem whose origins predate history. What precisely is the image that mathematicians called string theorists have invented to deduce a theory so "real" that it sustains them through decades in the desert of abstraction? String theory began with a problematic "truth" from quantum physics: in the quantum world, the smallest entity can be both a *particle* and a *wave* at the same time. Though no physicist claims to be able to explain how this enigma works, it is generally accepted to be fact. "What if," said the first string theorists, "what if the particle is not a dot, but a tightly-coiled *strand* of vibrating energy? What if everything in the universe forms a web of such strands? Would this not explain how all the infinitesimal particles could behave like vibrating waves?" According to Greene, ". . . the theory suggests that the microscopic landscape is suffused with tiny strings whose vibrational patterns orchestrate the evolution of the cosmos."[13]

Varieties in vibrations create the distinctive particles and gravitational forces that interact throughout the universe. Everything sounds logical at the outset, but as string theorists begin to pursue their subject to greater specificity, the little elastic loops of string begin to tie logic into knots. String theory requires that we expand our spatial vocabulary to include new dimensions "curled up" inside each string.[14] Moreover, actually to observe and measure the particles in which strings are curled would demand a particle-accelerator the size of the Milky Way.[15] Unfortunately, even imagination has its limits: the mind's eye can "see" only in the dimensions with which it is familiar. These inhibiting factors do not deter physicists any more than the absence of cameras with which to photograph God deter theology. Revelation, too, employs imagination to suggest the unimaginable, "What no eye has seen, nor ear heard, nor the human heart conceived . . ." (1 Cor 2:9).

Despite initial discouragement from other scientists and indifference from the rest of us, theoretical physicists work on. What keeps them going? Sheer, unshakable faith in one fundamental tenet of the yet-to-be-discovered "Theory of Everything": no matter how contradictory things sometimes appear, underneath all surface tangents and tangles everything is connected to everything else. Einstein's "general theory of relativity" (his explanation of gravity) describes the universe according to an orderly, geometric model; yet within each entity in the same universe, the quantum mechanics of Max Planck and his progeny discern "a frantic dance of subatomic particles."[16] Which picture of the world is accurate? Physicists say, "Both, but we just can't tell you how."

Ancient Greeks identified two such contradictory ruling forces in nature and in human psychology and invented two gods to express the truth they had observed. Apollo ruled the world of order, logic, and predictability, while Dionysus reigned in the wilderness of disorder and irrational passion. Wisely, the Greeks honored both gods by trying to maintain a balance between them in their culture.

String theorists hope to reconcile the disparity between the "rule of law" in the big world with the unpredictable chaos in the quantum world by a musical analogy. Individual instruments have limitations, depending on the vibrations of their strings. Each instrument appears to be limited by its shape and the number and timber of its strings, which produce some sounds and not others. But the limits are illusory, as we soon discover when the performer freely manipulates the strings to produce anything from a Mozart sonata to a jazz improvisation. This is an attractive metaphor for the combination of rule and freedom required to produce harmony in all spheres, but it doesn't begin to resolve all the new difficulties string theory raises.

Nevertheless, with supreme confidence in the laws of mathematics and the creativity of metaphor, Brian Greene and colleagues have pitched their tents in the desert of mathematical abstraction, believing that superstring theory will eventually show that the two scientific worlds of "classical" and "hard rock" are not incompatible. In fact, Greene is convinced that they require each other. "The marriage of the laws of the large and the small is not only happy, but inevitable."[17] Since string theory is still untestable, Greene's admirable ambition must be accepted for what it is—an act of faith.

Among the inspirations for this book has been my conviction that scientific metaphor can provide a solid foundation for faith to cope with the vicissitudes of contemporary spiritual life. As a mother and a therapist, Marion Goldstein has chosen to make this the theme of many of her poems, and in this case she invokes a scientific metaphor to fortify the faith of someone in a sadly familiar situation.

Gravity

*"Failure and disaster often foster the pre-conditions that
lead to a new evolutionary outburst."*
You are leaving him.
Broken like the stem of a rose
you are split in two.

Hanging by a thread in the garden
you are withering
under the weight
of accumulated loss
and fear the final fall
petals scattering on the ground.
You think your life is over
but trust the cosmic evolution.
The farther you travel
from the gravitational
pull of the dream
that has disintegrated
into nothing
but a fantasy
the lighter you will become
shedding the thorns
lighter and lighter
you can not escape
the stars
floating out of time
to greet you.

Marion Goldstein

The Eye of the Blackbird
Seeing into the Web of the Universe

Decades before the emergence of string theory, Jesuit scientist Teilhard de Chardin also combined faith and imagination to come to a vision that microtechnology had yet to reveal:

> We have gradually come to understand that no elemental thread in the Universe is wholly independent . . . of its neighboring threads. Each forms a part of a sheaf; and the sheaf in turn represents a higher order of thread in a still larger sheaf—and so on indefinitely.[18]

For both Teilhard and Brian Greene, faith in a Theory of Everything became the "eye of the blackbird," the lens with which both faith and science penetrate to "the heart of matter," where everything is connected to everything else.

Without attempting to comprehend the complexities of string theory or to extrapolate all its spiritual implications and analogies, I would like to focus on this one insight that so strongly supports and images the foundations of Christian spirituality: no particle of matter exists in isolation; every microscopic field of energy in the universe is a *society*. "Physicists have now probed the structure of matter to scales of about a billionth of a billionth of a meter and shown that everything encountered to date . . . consists of 'families' of quarks, electrons, and neutrinos."[19] Dominican theologian Mary Catherine Hilkert perceives this scientific fact as a teeming symbol of the Trinity itself:

> The mystery we describe as three diverse and equal persons in a mutual communion of love, is it not mirrored in the vision of a universe in which three trillion creatures with equal right to exist and equal need for each other are continually created and sustained in a mutual communion of love?[20]

The deeper science penetrates into the inner structure of the universe, the more its findings convince some theologians that not only humanity but all creation images a Trinitarian understanding of God. One thing we can understand about the mystery of the Trinity: God exists always and essentially in relationship. Therefore, human persons, created in the image of God, are "created to be persons in communion."[21] For most of us, this message has already been made so familiar as a theme of the Gospels that we have almost stopped hearing it. We need bolder homilies to recapture our attention. Fortunately, even those who have abandoned the churches acknowledge the authority of science. For them science provides a "parallel text" by demonstrating that need for communion is actually encoded into the fabric of the universe. Then, to a congregation whose economy thrives on competition, physics preaches an unwelcome sermon: nothing that exists needs to be *first;* everything that exists needs to be *mutual.*

Summarizing the work of liberation theologian Leonardo Boff, Elizabeth Johnson points out the relevance of Trinity to economic justice: ". . . the triune God whom we encounter in history as the origin, mediator, and driving force of liberation, *dwells as a community of love* wherein there is total equality amid mutuality and respect for differences."[22] The human community most truly fulfills its identity "in the image of God" when all its members are treated as equals, when attitudes and behavior reflect the mutuality in the Trinity's "community of love." Jesus treats us as equals when he invites us to his own awesome intimacy with the Father: ". . . you will know that I am in my Father, and you in me, and I in you" (John 14:20). Did Jesus not also promise that those who believed in him would have a capacity to do good equal to his own? "Very truly, I tell you, the one who believes in me will also do the works that I do and, in fact, will do greater works than these" (John 14:12). Is it really humility to decline so much of God's own power and freedom? Is it, perhaps, closer to cowardice to resist equal responsibility for God's world? String theory suggests that answers to such questions are not a private matter.

Inflections and Innuendoes
A Pentecost/Eucharist Experience

Each year on Pentecost, Christians celebrate two fundamental be-liefs that nourish their souls and inspire their choices all year long: the indwelling of the Holy Spirit and the glory and responsibility of membership in the Mystical Body of Christ. Our awareness of these mysteries is usually communicated through the readings and homilies at Eucharist. The tiny nugget of string theory that opens this chapter can provide the matrix for metaphors with which to probe these two mysteries. Christian artists have found the Third Person of the Blessed Trinity least amenable to graphic illustration and have, therefore, de-picted the Holy Spirit in terms of action: igniting conflagrations, stirring things up, inspiring new ideas.

> As the Source strikes the note,
> Humanity sings—
> The Holy Spirit is our harpist,
> And all strings
> Which are touched in Love
> Must sound.[23]
>
> *Mechtilde of Magdeburg*

Perhaps meditating on the vibrating strings of the universe as symbols of the Holy Spirit's action in the indestructible web of creation can generate hope at a time when many of us perceive our civilization to be "hanging by a thread."

Since the Middle Ages the most eloquent writers about the Holy Spirit have been women. Among the most poetic were the Rhineland mystics, who consistently addressed the Third Person as Sophia. Their eccentric imagery captures the action of the divine indwelling as source of human freedom:

> Sophia!
> You of the whirling wings,
> Circling encompassing
> Energy of God:
> You quicken the world in your clasp
>
> One wing soars in heaven
> One wing sweeps the earth
> And the third flies all around us
> Praise to Sophia!
> Let all the earth praise her![24]

>   *Hildegard of Bingen*

For the past three decades feminist theologians have unanimously approached the Spirit, not from the New Testament's Pentecost event, where the Spirit makes a dramatic entry as an external agitator, but from the Book of Wisdom's creation event, where the Spirit operates as an internal vivifier (Wis 7:24). Like Hildegard, feminists equate the Spirit with the figure of Wisdom in the Old Testament, who is always "she." Already they have developed a rich tradition of the divine Spirit who holds all things in being, not commandingly from without but dynamically from within (Wis 7:22; 8:1, 2-3, 9). Not unconsciously, perhaps, feminist verbs like "weaving," "connecting," "dialoguing" chime with the imagery scientists have chosen to characterize the flow of energy in the invisible web that engages even rocks and rivers in a program of cosmic altruism:

> The shapes and layers of rocks, sands, clays, and waters kept, and still keep, a vast, slow, dialogue of giving and receiving, each changing and being changed without pause.[25]

Like the physicists who capture the abstractions of string theory in a musical analogy, Rosemary Haughton describes the Holy Spirit as the great "choreographer" who leads "the dance of creation" from "oneness to diversity to the possibility of true union."[26] Feminists see the Holy Spirit's role in the creation and re-creation of the physical universe and of the human race as that of a persuasive community-builder. Elizabeth Johnson writes of the Spirit:

> One of her signature works is the creation of community. As Holy Spirit, God's own self-communication in grace, she vivifies human beings with divine life, consecrating them at their core and welding them into . . . a great intergenerational company of persons in the matrix of the natural world, *itself the original sacred community of life.*[27]

The first "public appearance" of the Holy Spirit in the Christian community makes one of the most theatrical scenes in the New Testament (Acts 2:1-4). With a wind so loud that it draws a huge crowd and flaming tongues that both terrify and fortify those gathered in the upper room, the noisy arrival of the Spirit contrasts sharply with the serene and inconspicuous presence of the Spirit in the Book of Wisdom, and also with the unobtrusive resurrection of Jesus. Taken together, these scenes resemble the contradictory modes of operation in the worlds of Einstein and Planck that continue to perplex physicists. Evidently, the Spirit, being herself the Theory of Everything, functions equally well in both.

And apparently the Holy Spirit has endowed Jesus' disciples with similar poise. Having absolutely no idea what will happen next, the little band steps out into the larger community. And what a community it is that the Holy Spirit has recruited for them!

> Now there were devout Jews from every nation under heaven living in Jerusalem. And at this sound the crowd gathered and was bewildered, because each one heard them speaking in the native language of each. Amazed and astonished, they asked, "Are not all these who are speaking Galileans? And how is it that we hear, each of us, in our own native language? Parthians, Medes, Elamites, and residents of Mesopotamia, Judea and Cappadocia, Pontus and Asia, Phrygia and Pamphylia, Egypt and the parts of Libya belonging to Cyrene, and visitors from Rome, both Jews and proselytes, Cretans and Arabs—in our own languages we hear them speaking about God's deeds of power." All were amazed and perplexed, saying to one another, "What does this mean?" (Acts 2:5-12).

It has taken twenty centuries for human technology to expose what it all meant: this scene is not an anomaly but a visible expression of an invisible fact: people—and species—of every nation under heaven, as well as the dust under their feet and the stars above their heads, are all one community whose native language, the breath of the Spirit, pulsates within and among them.

When only a bombastic Cotton Mather can rouse a congregation from complacency, the breath of the Spirit can reach gale-force intensity. Recently, in a single historic harangue, the howling winds of Hurricane Katrina shook American self-confidence to its roots and exposed the dark, tangled strings tying affluence to destitution and power to help-lessness. As vibrations of devastation and compassion rippled outward across a continent, arcane superstring theory assumed merciless clarity: everything that exists is bound up in closed loops of interdependence from which nothing escapes.

For how many years have most of us listened to the Pentecost readings with varying levels of indifference—until all the nations enumerated there moved from Jerusalem into our own backyards? And when they came, did we recognize their alien tongues as vibrations on the strings of an orchestra with which God has chosen to perform an intercontinental symphony? Or did we listen with deaf ears until each day brought word of new deaths and atrocities among the very nations assembled on Pentecost? Have we even now begun to pray for "God's deed of power" most needed in our time: a nation that can speak and hear the language of non-violence, which alone can repair the strands of creation's tattered web?

Peter's first words to the crowd exhibit a remarkable consciousness that he is empowered with the Spirit of God to address a community in which the same Spirit is working: "a great intergenerational company of persons in the matrix of the natural world." That intergenerational company includes the prophet Joel, whom Peter quotes:

> In the last days it will be, God declares,
> that I will pour out my Spirit upon all flesh,
>   and your sons and your daughters shall prophesy,
> and your young men shall see visions,
>   and your old men shall dream dreams.
> Even upon my slaves, both men and women,
>   in those days I will pour out my Spirit (Acts 2:17-18; Joel 3:1-5).

We have never needed, and do not need now, to understand the intricacies of string theory, to hear in it a reiteration in physical terms of these words to the first Christians—and even more tellingly to us. Modern science echoes Peter's message: the same energy pulses through the strands of all creation; the egalitarian Spirit of God is poured out on *all*. The Spirit recognizes no hierarchies; her extravagance leaves elitists with no one or nothing to "look down on." Better yet, for those who are willing to accept that Spirit, dreams and visions will open their eyes to unheard-of possibilities; the works of their imagination will know no limits.

All this is true even if string theory itself never reaches beyond the speculative stage. The contemporary relevance of the Pentecost event is clear as soon as we meditate deeply enough on the established facts of our global interdependency. These established facts lead scientists like Bohm and Davies to assert that space itself is an unbroken web of relationality in which quantum particles at opposite ends of the universe affect one another.[28] Christians have long been energized by a similar sense of solidarity and responsibility in the metaphor of the Mystical Body of Christ. We have always known, and are frequently reminded, that on Pentecost God revealed that "the full expression of 'the Christ' transcends the historical Jesus. God resurrected Jesus not just *for* his followers, but *in* his followers so that all of them participate at a mystical level in the risen body of Christ."[29]

Reading science as revelation of sacred truth becomes an invitation to broaden and deepen the concept of the Mystical Body to include not only all Christians but all creatures, the earth itself, and the cosmos sacralized by the Jesus-event. According to Karl Rahner, "the Resurrection of Jesus introduced a new force of transformation into the earth itself."[30] Technology has converted the scientific community into believers in the power of even microscopic particles to change things. Thinking of this power as a metaphor for the impact of the Incarnation should both inspire and embarrass those of us who chronically complain of helplessness.

People of faith, discouraged by the apparent triumph of evil in our world, should take heart—and take pause—long enough to meditate on their traditional beliefs in light of new scientific information and long enough to re-examine their quotidian choices in light of their global impact. Fortunately, science persuades us that that impact is more real than apparent. With this understanding, the indwelling of the Holy Spirit is neither a figure of speech nor an optional adjunct to a humanistic lifestyle. The Spirit indwelling in the living Body of Christ is the driving force that endows all individual acts of goodness with cumulative value, including the most interior movements of will—value not only "in God's eyes" but in their contribution to the ultimate well-being of distant strangers and atheists.

For Americans in particular, because individualism is so much a part of our national character, it will be especially painful to surrender some of that individualism to embrace the vision of science with the ardor of faith as Teilhard did: "each of us is connected by all the fibers of our being—material, organic, psychic, mental—with everything around us . . . all human beings together are in the process of forming a new unity, *higher than that of a collection of individuals.*"[31] Because the Spirit's web of creation is not a static structure, a dynamic process of renovation is constantly in play. Many times our confidence in the Spirit's role in the process will be shaken when undeniably destructive forces with global consequences are more evident than any "vibrations" from acts of genuine virtue. In this century the unprecedented acceleration of religiously motivated violence directed at civilians delivers a terrifying example of the apparent ascendancy of evil. In this situation we might humbly reflect that perhaps we are living through the "demolition phase" of a New Jerusalem and willingly surrender to the wrecking ball anything in our own hearts that obstructs transformation.

In spite of a half century or more of instruction, some Catholics continue to equate the term "Body of Christ" exclusively with the Eucharist and even with the phrase "Real Presence." Since the Second Vatican Council, the church's eucharistic theology has reflected evolutionary science by focusing on Eucharist, not as a simple presence, but as a dynamic event.[32] The event that the eucharistic ritual celebrates is the transformation of humanity into the Body of Christ. As food is transformed into flesh and flesh into energy, thought, laughter, passion, so the community of believers are transformed into one body, the presence of Christ in the world. This is the tradition.

Contemporary process theologians take it further. Some go so far as to integrate the Eucharist into "the entire universe as an organic community of interlocked events."[33] Teilhard de Chardin's prayer "Mass over the World" is a famous example of how a scientist's understanding of the Incarnation's impact on the earth itself inspired him to offer a unique Eucharist at which he had no access to the usual equipment for the sacrifice. Standing in a trench on a bloody battlefield, he prayed:

Since today, Lord, I your Priest, have neither bread nor wine, nor altar, I shall spread my hands over the whole universe and take its immensity as the matter of my sacrifice. . . . Let creation repeat to itself, again today, and tomorrow, and until the end of time, so long as the transformation has not run its full course, the divine saying: "This is my body."[34]

Teilhard's prayer, lifted up during World War I and not published until after his death in 1953, has been repeated in essence by thousands of "priestly people" on mountains, in forests, and in "ungodly" venues transformed by Teilhard's vision into sacred altars. In itself, the prayer is a perfect example of how vibrations from an infinitesimal particle can move a world.

While Teilhard's "Mass" expands the moment of consecration, Bernard Lee's profound and moving reflection on the Real Presence breaks the traditional private thanksgiving after Holy Communion wide open:

Whatever shapes and creates me in any way is present to and in me. . . . Whatever in the world nourishes my becoming is present to me. . . . Those who have contributed to who I am are more present than people in the room with me.[35]

In Lee's last sentence many of us will recognize experiences we ourselves have had (independent of any scientific or theological influence), experiences of the presence of our beloved dead, either with us or within us, during Eucharist.

One purpose of these pages has been to demonstrate that spirituality informed by science need not relinquish traditional sacraments and symbols. In fact, Whitehead has warned: "Those who cannot combine reverence for their symbols with freedom of revision must ultimately decay either from anarchy or from . . . slow atrophy."[36] Whitehead's warning will assist Christian theologians in preaching a spirituality of global interdependence to congregations who have been nourished for millennia by metaphors of relationality like Trinity and Mystical Body of Christ. In my experience, the "new cosmology" takes deepest root among Christians who have related to the universe as a sacrament all their lives. Their deepest joy is in finding that scientific data resonate with personal faith experiences to make the familiar astonishing again.

My Interior Landscape

Who am I?
I am a child of the universe
    a woman of earth
    a creature of God
I stand in awe of the ever
    expanding universe
        birthing a nursery of galaxies,
        compressing the weight of a billion stars
            the size of our sun
            into a minute black hole
            the size of my thumb,
        midwiving brown dwarves
                whose light will never sparkle
            like the stars that accompany
            planet Earth on her rounds.
I marvel at the elves of lightning
    at the edge of space
    seen by the naked eye
    if eyes are open in that one-thousandth of a second
    gazing sixty miles sky high.
If the vastness of outer space
    is replicated within one atom
How much more the immensity of God
    is found in me
    flooding my whole being with divine mystery.

Late have I loved thee
Ancient God, ever new.
You have found me again
    gifted me
    while taking off my shoe.
You come at the most unexpected moments
    but upon reflection
    I realize
    you come as you promised
    when I love another
    as you have loved me.
Take birth often, O cosmic Christ,
    in the vastness of my interior landscape
    and let me in on the divine secrets of your universe. Amen.

Mary McGuinness, O.P.

All those who search for truth, whether in books, in atom-smashers, or in prayer have sudden encounters like those described above, where they are simply *found*. It happens to agnostic scholars and scientists as well as to illiterate peasants. The struggle to name such an event has led the learned to some amusing linguistic anomalies, as we have seen in earlier chapters. But one such event can sustain faith for a lifetime.

Untitled

Moving across the blank page
the sound of my pencil
creates a silence
the wake of a tiny ship.

The silence becomes a person
more real to me than myself
a companion looking over my shoulder
smiling a little at the poem
that has ceased to matter.

Nothing I shall ever write
can be more true
more trustworthy
than this faceless presence
beside
　　beyond
　　　　inexorably within.

The wise ones called you Unpronounceable.
He called you Abba.
Now they tell us to call you
Quantum Vacuum, Empty Fullness.
Whatever.

Language neither creates nor destroys
this moment
this moving stillness
whose white sails carry me
　　through darkest waters
　　　　unerringly home.

Elizabeth Michael Boyle, O.P.

NOTES

[1] Gjertrud Schnakenberg, "Supernatural Love," in *Supernatural Love: Poems 1976–1992* (New York: Farrar Straus and Giroux, 2000).

[2] Diarmuid O'Murchu, *Quantum Theology: Spiritual Implications of the New Physics* (New York: Crossroad, 2003) 49.

[3] Barbara Brown Taylor, *The Luminous Web: Essays on Science and Religion* (Cambridge: Cowley Publications, 2000) 74.

[4] Stanley Kunitz, *The Wild Braid: A Poet Reflects on a Century in the Garden* (New York: W. W. Norton, 2005) 100.

[5] Pierre Teilhard de Chardin, *Toward the Future,* trans. Rene Hague (New York: Harcourt Brace Jovanovich, 1975) 214.

[6] Elizabeth Johnson, *Women, Earth, and Creator Spirit* (New York: Paulist Press, 1993) 36.

[7] Although Brian Greene routinely refers to the history of string theory as comprising the last two decades of the twentieth century, his own "Brief History" chronicles intermittent progress since 1968. *The Elegant Universe: Superstrings, Hidden Dimensions, and the Quest for the Ultimate Theory* (New York: W. W. Norton, 1999) 136–140.

[8] Testimony from leading specialists in the field attesting to this introduces the documentary *Elegant Universe,* written and directed by Julia Cort and Joseph McMaster, based on *The Elegant Universe* by Brian Greene (Nova Productions, 2003).

[9] Ibid.

[10] So named by Ed Witten, string theory pioneer.

[11] Nima Arkami-Hamed, "E=mc² Explained," *Einstein's Big Idea Homepage.*

[12] Greene, *Elegant Universe,* 17.

[13] Ibid., 135.

[14] Rick Groleau, "Imagining Other Dimensions," *The Elegant Universe Homepage.*

[15] Peter Tyson, "A Sense of Scale," *The Elegant Universe Homepage.*

[16] Greene, *Elegant Universe.*

[17] Ibid., 4.

[18] Teilhard de Chardin, cited in Ursula King, *The Life and Vision of Teilhard de Chardin* (Maryknoll, NY: Orbis Books, 1996) 39.

[19] Greene, *Elegant Universe,* 17.

[20] Mary Catherine Hilkert, O.P., *Imago Dei: Does the Symbol Have a Future?* (Santa Clara: Santa Clara Lectures, 2002) vol. 8, no. 3, 18.

[21] John Paul II, "Mulieris Dignitatem: Apostolic Letter on the Dignity and Vocation of Women," *Origins,* vol. 18, no. 17 (6 October 1998) no. 6.268.

[22] Elizabeth Johnson, C.S.J., *She Who Is: The Mystery of God in Feminist Theological Discourse* (New York: Crossroad, 1993) 208. Leonardo Boff, *Trinity and Society* (Maryknoll, NY: Orbis Press, 1998).

[23] Mechtilde of Magdeburg, in *Women in Praise of the Sacred: 43 Centuries of Spiritual Poetry by Women,* ed. Jane Hirshfield (New York: HarperCollins, 1994) 93.

[24] Hildegard of Bingen, "Antiphon for Divine Wisdom," trans. Barbara Newman, in Hirshfield, *43 Centuries,* 67.

[25] Rosemary Haughton, *The Passionate God* (New York: Paulist Press, 1981) 22.

[26] Ibid., 54.

[27] Elizabeth Johnson, *Truly Our Sister* (New York: Continuum, 2003) 306.

[28] Cited by O'Murchu in *Quantum Theology*, 57.

[29] David Impastato, *Upholding Mystery: An Anthology of Christian Poetry* (New York: Oxford University Press, 1997) 277.

[30] Karl Rahner, "Easter: A Faith That Loves the Earth," in *The Great Church Year* (New York: Crossroad, 1993) 195.

[31] Teilhard, cited in King, *The Life and Vision of Teilhard de Chardin*, 54.

[32] See, for example, Edward Schillebeeckx, *The Eucharist* (New York: Sheed and Ward, 1968).

[33] Bernard Lee, "The Lord's Supper," in *Religious Experience and Process Theology: The Pastoral Implications of a Major Modern Movement*, ed. Harry James Cargas and Bernard Lee (New York: Paulist Press, 1976) 255.

[34] Teilhard de Chardin, "The Priest," in *Writings in Time of War* (London: Collins, 1968) 205–207.

[35] Lee, "The Lord's Supper," 286–287.

[36] Alfred North Whitehead, *Symbolism: Its Meaning and Effect* (New York: Capricorn Books, 1959) 88.

Chapter Seven

REFLECTIONS ON SPACE
EXPLORATION

*"The whole universe together participates in the divine goodness
and represents it better than any single being whatsoever."*
(Thomas Aquinas, Theologian)[1]

*"When I have a terrible need of . . . shall I say the word? . . . of religion,
I go out at night and paint the stars."*
(Vincent Van Gogh, Artist)[2]

*"It was science that drove me to the conclusion
that the world is much more complicated than can be explained by
science. It is only through the supernatural
that I can understand the mystery of existence."*
(Alan Sandage, Astronomer)[3]

*"If we could actually feel ourselves sliding through space
at the rate of thirty kilometers per second,
would we still pester God about good weather for the family reunion?"*
(Barbara Brown Taylor, Professor/Preacher)[4]

*" . . . star dust
scattered in our stones
seeded in our bones
. . . the itch of memory
calling us to our source."*
(Marion Goldstein, Poet)[5]

"As for the future,
your task is not to foresee it
but to enable it."
(Antoine de Saint-Exupéry, Aviator)[6]

"Everything there is
is the trapeze,
no net."
(Frederick Seidel, Poet)[7]

Newscasts from outer space exhibit two phenomena which, taken together, comprise a consistent paradox. On the one hand, interstellar satellite explorers often deliver photographic confirmation for the existence of places and events that, until now, were confined to poetry, science fiction, and other realms of pure imagination. On the other hand, the same astrophysical technologies routinely generate data that contradict or bring into question places and events that have long been accepted as "scientific facts."[8] Imagination appears to be more reliably accurate than science. The fact that professional researchers publicize their earlier mistakes should strengthen rather than weaken the public's trust in their methods and motives. Even so, non-scientists can be forgiven a certain guilty delight when incidents show that the imaginations of poets and artists have stolen the march on scientists' painstaking intellectual labor.

To begin with a whimsical example: Back in 1943, when the first American edition of Antoine de Saint-Exupéry's *Little Prince* was published, readers smiled at the most unique and endearing feature of his imaginary home. On tiny "Asteroid B12" the fictional hero could watch forty-four sunsets in a single day. On July 14, 2005, *Nature Magazine* reported a newly discovered world in outer space consisting of one planet orbiting a sun-like star with two other stars in the planet's own orbit. And what did astrophysicists hail as the most unique feature of the "new" planetary system? Every day imaginary citizens of this new world could enjoy the phenomenal spectacle of multiple sunrises and sunsets.[9]

Cosmology confirms many other poetic insights. By now every schoolchild knows that, physically, everything that exists originated as star dust, that all the elements essential to life were once synthesized inside dying stars and then scattered into space.[10] For students of American literature, the idea is doubly familiar, for years before Edwin Hubble's explorations paved the way for Big Bang theory,[11] Walt Whitman's most famous poem stated boldly: "A leaf of grass is no less than the journey-work of the stars." As Brian Swimme observes, "You could say that Walt Whitman had a 'deep memory' of where he came from."[12]

Perhaps the most numerous predictions of scientific technology have been the futuristic inventions of science-fiction novelists and screenwriters. At the end of the nineteenth century, for example, when experiments in motion photography were first being attempted, H. G. Wells' fiction featured *The Time Machine* and *The Accelerator*, which anticipated cinematic feats that technology achieved decades later, such as the capacity to see backward in time and to capture the "invisible" life-cycles of microscopic flora and fauna in slow motion.[13]

Creative intuition of facts before they are discovered by science is not reserved for literary artists. As one example out of many I could cite, consider the recent testimony from outer space that the "music of the spheres," the Pythagorean metaphor that has inspired great composers throughout the ages, is no figment of human imagination. As music critic John Rockwell commented, "Who knew? All those philosophers and scientists, and theoreticians who believed in the ancient Music of the Spheres were on to something. There is such a music, and it's the note of B-Flat."[14] Rockwell refers to the fact that in 2003 astronomers using the Hubble telescope registered a "cosmic hum" emanating from black holes with "a frequency equivalent to a B-flat which their instruments calculated to be 57 tones below middle C."[15] Among musicologists, this news from outer space has sparked an Internet quest for the emotional and aesthetic significance of B-Flat comparable to the physicists' search for the Theory of Everything.[16] Of more interest to astronomers than the exact musical key of these sounds is evidence that they are influencing events in distant galaxy clusters. Sonic explosions from black holes, astronomers now speculate, actually "orchestrate" the birth of new stars.[17] Poet Michael Horowitz chose to speak for the nameless extraterrestrial musician, fantasizing a first-person reply to astronomers:

> A supermassive ghostly Robeson robed in nothingness,
> I serenade the void from the heart of Perseus cluster,
> Underhumming the underpinnings of the galaxies in B flat.
> "Smoke Gets in Your Eyes" at 57 octaves below Middle C.
> Not even God hears me.

But any one of these icy nights beneath the warbling stars,
Those shards of horns long shivered that still take solos,
If you close your eyes you can almost sense my presence,
Blowing the antisong of the antispheres.[18]

Though characters in science fiction have been strolling the skies for centuries, it is only within the past four decades that real men and women and their robotic surrogates have actually traveled there. Not even science fiction ever anticipated the current volume of human activity on this "last frontier." Since 1958, when the first spacecraft, aptly named "Pioneer," reached toward earth's moon for a mere seventy-seven seconds, over two hundred space missions have set out for earth's moon and the planets, not counting shuttle flights to the International Space Station.[19] Space missions range from photographic observation, to testing new technologies, to gathering debris from the Big Bang, to SETI (Search for Extra-Terrestrial Intelligence). Journeys have lasted from under a minute to over years, and in several cases space vehicles and satellite instruments are still living out "life sentences" in orbit. Only a dozen astronauts have walked in space or on the surface of the moon, yet space exploration has become so commonplace that at any given moment, unless the event proves catastrophic, neither launch nor splashdown merits front-page coverage.

What has all this activity to do with pedestrian spirituality? More than one spiritual writer has observed that all spirituality is grounded in *gratitude*. With profound gratitude, I like to think of the astronauts and their support teams of engineers, scientists, mechanics, and computer geeks as a community of secular contemplatives, steadily elevating the consciousness of our race. Moreover, we can draw inspiration from the hidden life of these selfless laborers in a vast, invisible vineyard from which generations yet unborn will someday drink strange, medicinal wines. Meantime, for people of faith, the exotic harvest of information space pioneers are reaping from intergalactic fields provides a vast new library of revelatory texts for our reflection.

Looking Outward, Seeing Backward

We are the first humans to live with an empirical view of the origin of the universe. We are the first humans to look into the night sky and see the birth of the stars, the birth of galaxies, the birth of the cosmos as a whole. Our future as a species will be forged within this story of the world.[20]

Exploration into outer space has provided us with two ways to "see backward" in time to the very first moments of creation: telescopic photography and intergalactic archeology. Before we consider how the "time travel" of telescopic photography works, a simple description of how every telescope functions offers us an immediate metaphor for our search for God.

> All telescopes, large or small, cheap or expensive, are built with the same goal in mind—to gather as much light as possible from a target object, and magnify that light. Notice that the first priority of the telescope is to gather light. . . .[21]

The first object of our search is to gather light from a text, a personal encounter, a natural phenomenon, life situation, or historical event that *reflects* the target. Unlike the telescope, human intelligence does not magnify the light; it reduces it to a brightness that human nature can tolerate. Hence, the primary lens is always metaphor.

But the journey backward in time that the telescope and its cameras provide is enabled, not by poetic metaphor, but by mathematic reality. Because it takes an image light years to move through interstellar space from the object to the telescopic lens, whenever a camera moves outward in space, it captures a target eons away from it. The speed of light, 670 million miles per hour, is the established mathematical fact that explains how the Hubble Space Telescope performs a feat that used to belong in the realm of fantasy: to snap a photograph of the cosmos in the instant after the Big Bang. In fact, on February 12, 2003, such a photograph actually appeared on the first page of the *New York Times* under the startling headline "Cosmos Sits for Early Portrait, Gives Up Secrets."[22]

Astronomers hailed Hubble as the new king of history's audacious paparazzi: "The most detailed and precise map yet produced of the universe just after its birth confirms the Big Bang theory in triumphant detail and opens new chapters in the early history of the cosmos."[23] Though for most of us this photo seemed like many others in Hubble's growing gallery, astrophysicists recognized in the image "a seamless and consistent history of the universe from its first few seconds to the present . . . a rite of passage for cosmology from philosophical uncertainty to precision."[24]

By bringing the Big Bang into our living rooms, technology demolished distances of space and time and made the event seem both historical and very personal. We are all familiar with the psychological process whereby an event in the present ignites remembrance of a long-forgotten moment and motivates us to action in the present. Psychologist Dana Zohar suggests that the intimate connectedness of everything that exists extends human memory into "quantum memory," that is, remembrance of cosmic events:

> Through the process of quantum memory, where the wave patterns created by past experiences merge in the brain's quantum system with wave patterns created by present experience, my past is always with me. It exists not as a "memory," a finished and closed fact that I can recall, but as a living presence that partially defines what I am now. The wave patterns of the past are taken up and woven into now, relived afresh at each moment as something that has been, but also as something that is now being.[25]

For me personally, publication of Hubble's portrait of the infant cosmos triggered a conversation with two old portraits and put me in touch with my deceased mother in a new way. The episode may or may not be an example of "quantum memory."

Oval Portraits

Side by side on the shelf
stand two portraits of one woman
book-ending seven decades of wisdom
no volume can contain.

Both candid and withholding
the gaze of the little girl
in the sepia-toned oval
penetrates more deeply
than the self-assured triumph

of the matriarch celebrating
her golden wedding year.

Again and again over time
probing these ageless features
I search in vain for my own.
Dusting the miniature frame
and stroking the dark straight hair
I fail to unlock the tiny fist or
the secrets behind that pensive stare.

"Do you ever think of me?"
I question my child-mother.
"Do you feel a heartbeat
tapping the egg nested
in the ancient family tree,
hear leaves stirring the layered ruffles
of your quaint starched dress?

"Are you the strange dark energy still
smoldering in four Irish-American sons
twenty-six grandchildren
twenty-five—and counting—
pink, brown and honey-colored
great grandchildren
and one childless daughter

whose voice stammers
your unuttered poems
into the ears of strangers?
Is it you—or myself—
or everything unborn within me
that your eyes keep me searching for?

"If one distant lens can translate
vibrations from the cosmic birth-cry
into the photograph of a moment
thirteen billion years in the past
cannot the burning lens of this oval portrait
capture the star of your infant soul
exploding now into song?"

Elizabeth Michael Boyle, O.P.

Meditating on current events in the context of quantum memory can not only enrich our poetic imaginations; it should also expand our experience of timelessness and of solidarity, not only with the needs of the living but also with the strength of the dead.

Widening the Eye of the Blackbird

The catechism of the new cosmology begins with three very basic questions to which children used to have the answers: "Where do we come from?" "Are we alone?" "Where are we going?"[26] Scientists believe that their laboratories have already yielded the answer to the first question. Physically, everything that exists—human and non-human, single-celled and multi-celled, sentient and senseless—all descend from one common ancestor, the fiery kernel of the Big Bang. And we now have the technology to administer a cosmic paternity test. Scattered on the surfaces of stars, planets, and comets, detritus from the Big Bang offers a fairly uncontaminated source for DNA samples that can trace us back to our one faceless ancestor.

Deeper answers to the three basic questions require cooperation among many dedicated professionals with different specialties. First, deep-space photographers map an atlas of time and space with stunning surface photos of the cosmic landscape. Next, from the most promising sites identified by telescopic photography, astrobiologists and astrophysicists gather samples for genetic analysis. Without leaving the ground, these twenty-first century explorers journey to comets and planets and dispatch robotic archeologists to gather and store genetic samples. Then, in earthbound laboratories, thousands of researchers conduct comparative analysis of DNA samples from the interplanetary materials, while still others simulate the Big Bang event by biochemical synthesis, that is, test-tube evolution. This is not science fiction. Already a team of astrophysicists in a NASA program called Stardust Mission have successfully collected a sample from the comet Wild 2 and their robotic surrogates have returned to earth with their treasure.[27]

Meantime, another army of curious scientists is focused on gathering evidence to address the second question: "Are we alone?" In the absence of physical evidence of life on other planets, scientists take both sides. On the one hand, many reason that the sheer size and complexity of the universe argues against the probability that conditions for sustaining life have occurred on only one small planet.[28] On the other hand, the daunting number of elements and conditions that need to converge to sustain biological organisms convinces other scientists that the search for extraterrestrial life, and especially intelligent life, is futile. As usual, Teilhard de Chardin takes his stand on the side of the greater possibility, suggesting that earth is not the only place worthy of divine attention: "In a universe in which we can no longer seriously entertain the idea that thought is an exclusively terrestrial phenomenon, Christ must no longer be *constitutionally* restricted in his operation to mere redemption of our planet."[29]

In the absence of any immediate urgency for us to settle this question, we can enjoy the luxury of simply meditating on how the possibility of extraterrestrial brothers and sisters might expand our image of God. A hundred years ago a gentle Victorian poet showed us the way. Alice Meynell envisioned an interplanetary epiphany in which alien creatures introduce each other to their unique Christs. The poet does not show the assembled creatures proselytizing or trying to convert each other. Nor does she intimate that the sole mission of other Christs to other planets would have to be to "save" them.[30] She suggests that extraterrestrial intelligence, when and if it is encountered, will be a revelatory event in the evolution of theology. Though old-fashioned in poetic form, Alice Meynell's futuristic speculation on the million revelations awaiting us in outer space provokes many challenging questions. Without preaching, the poet subtly chides our human proclivity to reduce God to our own dimensions and invites us to reverence every manifestation of The Other. It was this poem, which I read as a teenager, that first attracted me to a fusion of poetry, science, and spirituality that has become a lifelong fascination.

Christ in the Universe

> With this ambiguous earth
> His dealings have been told us. These abide:
> The signal to a maid
> The lesson, and the young Man crucified.
>
> But not a star of all
> The innumerable host of stars has heard
> How He administered this terrestrial ball.
> Our race have kept their Lord's entrusted Word.

Of His earth-visiting feet
None knows the secret, cherished, perilous,
The terrible, shamefast, frightened, whispered, sweet
Heart-shattering secret of His way with us.

No planet knows that this
Our wayside planet, carrying land and wave,
Love and life multiplied, and pain and bliss,
Bears, as chief treasure, one forsaken grave.

Nor in our little day,
May His devices with the heavens be guessed,
His pilgrimage to thread the Milky Way
Or His bestowals there be manifest.

But in the eternities,
Doubtless we shall compare together, hear
A million Gospels, in what guise
He trod the Pleiades, the Lyre, the Bear.

O be prepared, my soul!
To read the inconceivable, to scan
The million forms of God those stars unroll
When, in our turn, we show to them a Man.[31]

Alice Meynell

Most of us will never need to endure the physical rigors of space exploration or the psychological rigors of colonization by extraterrestrial others. But should we ever encounter or be encountered by them, the ones best prepared for the event will be those who have already developed appreciation for and sensitivity to the diverse life-forms on our own planet. It sounds whimsical, perhaps, or even eccentric to suggest that space exploration is contributing to spiritual consciousness by preparing the way for fellowship with extraterrestrials. Isn't this kind of talk thinly disguised escapism? Shouldn't we concentrate on the needs of our earthly brothers and sisters? In my experience, in fact, those who are the most concerned about human needs are also the most concerned about the earth itself, about racial and cultural minorities, and the most open to the truth in all religions. Ecotheology readies the soul for exotheology.

At the present time, scientists believe the answer to "Are we alone?" will be found on the planet Mars, the most likely candidate for housing extraterrestrial life. In 2003, NASA joined an international fleet of space-craft, the first exploratory voyage of the twenty-first century, headed for "the red planet." Ever since, two robotic rovers, Spirit and Opportunity, have been scouring the surface of Mars for signs that organic life could have made a home there. Mars probes are intent, above all, on finding water. Water, more than any other element, including stardust, it seems, establishes an immediate spiritual connection between humanity and everything else in the natural world.

Privileged to Be

Snow is privileged to be one of water's expressions of God.
The ocean is privileged to be one of water's expressions of God.
Waterfalls are privileged to be one of water's expressions of God.
Women are 75% water. Men are 70% water.
Babies are 90% water.
We are privileged to be water's expression of God.

Mary C. McGuinness, O.P.

Poets since the beginning of time have used thirst as the symbol for the deepest human desire:

My soul thirsts for you . . .
as in a dry and weary land
where there is no water (Ps 63:1).

And the poet of the Fourth Gospel chose living water as the ulti-mate fulfillment of that desire: "The water that I will give will become in them a spring of water gushing up to eternal life" (John 4:14). Paradoxically, the same news media that carry exciting photos of the latest triumphs of human ingenuity in outer space also carry shocking photos of earthly inhabitants dying of thirst because their water supplies have been destroyed or polluted by human violence. Michael Morwood suggests that the intellectual and spiritual fire that fuels scientific ex-ploration should have a practical outcome: "Some people die of thirst, but others live by it: scientists, poets, mystics, and those blessed ones who thirst for justice and do something about it."[32] Similar sentiments disturb anyone with an ear for irony.

Thirst

If we ever find water on Mars
will it be potable?
Will it slake the thirst that drove us here
and the greater one that drives us back

To that cool well by the cooler woman
who looked for love in all the wrong places
and found it at last in the eyes of a stranger
who asked her for a drink?[33]

Is this what we're really looking for
—or running from—when we
wander interplanetary deserts
and plunder subatomic jungles

where it's safer to search
without the least chance
of meeting the eyes of some stranger
who asks for more than a drink?

Elizabeth Michael Boyle, O.P.

Inflections and Innuendoes
A Timeless Experience

Perhaps the most startling scientific news to conclude the twentieth century was the discovery that the composition of the entire cosmos, including humanity, consists of four percent atoms and ninety-six percent "dark" matter and energy.[34] Cosmologists continually tweak the figures, but all agree that "nothing" outweighs everything by a huge margin. What exactly is dark matter? Though physicists are certain *that it is*, they cannot yet say *what it is*. According to Brian Greene, this "invisible bath immersing the universe . . . does not participate in the processes of nuclear fusion that power the stars . . . (and therefore) does not give off light (and hence) . . . is invisible to the astronomer's telescope."[35] Other physicists define dark energy as the "mysterious force that accounts for a gravitational pull that affects the behavior of stars . . . in ways that cannot be accounted for."[36] Still others are convinced that "there is unquestionable evidence that everything we see is governed by that which we now cannot."[37] Since the beginnings of recorded wisdom, mystics have come to a similar conclusion about spiritual reality.

> . . . mystery and manifestations
> arise from the same source.
> This source is called darkness.
> Darkness within darkness.
> The gateway to all understanding.[38]

Meditating on dark matter, Marion Goldstein followed the metaphor from astrophysics, to the delivery room, to the cemetery, exploring the redemptive darkness of personal tragedy.

Luster from Another Realm

Seventy-two percent
of the universe
is missing.

Devoid of matter
like Jupiter and Australia
foliage or lettuce

is the unbound ocean
of black dazzle
that pillow for the cosmos

incapable of radiating
or reflecting
light

it is flashing
in and out
of existence

on luster
borrowed
from another realm.

The way the baby
flashed from my flooded womb
in a great tidal wave

of blood
and was gone
they said

he could not breathe
in this world
of oxygen and medicine

they said
he was not meant to be

how endure
the hole of pain
your own exploding star

and now
my dear friend
your husband's ashes

pour
through your fingers
matter is marrying matter

under the arborvitae
in the garden
those forty years

swallowed in the quicksand
of New York Hospital
are even now

transforming
like molten gold
and devotion

infuses
invisible particles
of the fifth dimension

and like moonlight
passing through
the glass pane

of a locked window
it shines.[39]

Marion Goldstein

Among all the images in outer space, stars endow poets and philosophers with the richest cornucopia of sacred metaphor—and, thanks
to science, of paradox. These traditional emblems of certitude and con-
stancy turn out to be in a continual throes of death and destruction.
By the time its glow is seen on earth, a star's self-immolation has been
complete for eons. In a desperate struggle between gravity pulling it in
and nuclear energy pushing it out, the star consumes itself in order to
exist.[40] These ancient symbols of supernatural light are actually locked
in constant conflict with "black holes."[41] Yet black holes, into which
defeated stars collapse, are in fact white-hot sources of incredible energy. As Diarmuid O'Murchu comments: "To put it philosophically,
the forces of death may be driving the forces of life."[42] O'Murchu calls
this alternating extinction and transformation on the cosmic landscape
"the evolutionary equivalents of Calvary and Resurrection."[43] Science
has revealed that a parallel text to the Gospels has been scrawled across
the firmament since before the beginning of time. And what message
does the universe echo? Creation and self-renewal demand continual
kenosis, in imitation of the Creator's extravagant, self-giving love.

Choices

Astrophysics describes two ways
for a star to die.

The one, slowly, steadily:
a slender flame licking upward
devouring night's unresisting taper
leaving neither offspring nor residue.

Eventually, bereft of oxygen
consumed in self-absorption
it fizzles in its own fat
sputters and dies
disturbing the outer darkness
not at all.

The other, instantaneously:
supernova exploding outward into the universe
giving itself to the darkness
risking everything, withholding nothing
radiating for miles and light-millennia
sudden death detonating fecundity
propagating the night with a thousand children.
Even after self-immolation
in excess of light,
it re-ignites a forest of candles
shivering in the draft we dare to call
"Enlightenment."[44]

Elizabeth Michael Boyle, O.P.

NOTES

[1] Thomas Aquinas, *Summa Theologica*, q. 47, art. 1.

[2] Quoted in Lynn Gamwell, *Exploring the Invisible: Art, Science, and the Spiritual* (Princeton: Princeton University Press, 2002) 51.

[3] Alan Sandage, assistant to and successor of Edwin Hubble, astronomer who discovered quasars. Quoted in Michael Reagan, ed., *The Hand of God: Thoughts and Images Reflecting the Spirit of the Universe* (Philadelphia: Templeton Foundation Press, 1999) 21.

[4] Barbara Brown Taylor, *The Luminous Web: Essays on Science and Religion* (Cambridge: Cowley Publications, 2000) 90–91.

[5] Marion Goldstein, "Matter: Dark and Light," in *Psalms for the Cosmos* (Johnstown, OH: Pudding House Press, 2003).

[6] Antoine de Saint-Exupéry, *The Wisdom of the Sands,* trans. Stuart Gilbert (Chicago: University of Chicago Press, 1979, 1950).

[7] Frederick Seidel, "The Last Remaining Angel," in *The Cosmos Poems* (New York: Farrar, Straus and Giroux, 2000).

[8] Newspapers seem to delight in headlining challenges to science almost as much as challenges to religion. For example, "Galaxy Drift Challenges Ideas About Universe Evolution"; "Hubble Discovers Black Holes in Unexpected Places"; "Astronomers Have Found a Spiral Galaxy That May Be Spinning to a Different Cosmic Drummer."

[9] John Noble Wilford, "Discovery of a First: A World with Three Suns," *New York Times* (15 July 2005) F1.

[10] Marcello Gleiser, *The Dancing Universe: From Creation Myths to the Big Bang* (New York: Dutton Penguin, 1997) 295.

[11] Hubble's law, published in 1929, measured the speed of galaxies receding from each other. This information eventually led to the Big Bang theory, which was confirmed in 1965 by the discovery of cosmic microwave radiation.

[12] Brian Swimme, "Comprehensive Compassion," interview in *What Is Enlightenment Online Magazine* (Spring/Summer, 2001).

[13] Oliver Sachs, "Speed," *The New Yorker* (23 August 2004) 60.

[14] John Rockwell, "Move Over Middle C: The Speculative Case for the Cosmic B Flat," *New York Times* (30 January 2004) E5.

[15] Dennis Overbye, "Music of the Heavens Turns Out to Sound a Lot Like B Flat," *New York Times* (16 September 2003) F3; "Songs of the Galaxies and What They Mean," *New York Times* (3 August 2004) F1.

[16] Rockwell lists scholarly tomes and websites where readers may join the pursuit.

[17] Overbye, "Songs of the Galaxies."

[18] Michael Horowitz, cited in Overbye, "Songs of the Galaxies."

[19] Melanie Melton Knocke, *From Blue Moons to Black Holes: A Basic Guide to Astronomy, Outer Space, and Space Exploration* (Amherst, NY: Prometheus Books, 2005) 225–298.

[20] Brian Swimme, *The Universe Is a Green Dragon,* quoted in Reagan, *The Hand of God,* 156.

[21] Knocke, *From Blue Moons to Black Holes,* 174.

[22] Dennis Overbye, "Cosmos Sits for Early Portrait, Gives Up Secrets," *The New York Times* (12 February 2003) A1.

[23] Ibid.

[24] Ibid.

[25] Dana Zohar, *The Quantum Self: Human Nature and Consciousness Defined by the New Physics* (New York: William Morrow, 1990) 145.

[26] Charles Siebert, "The Genesis Project," *New York Times Magazine* (26 September 2004) 54.

[27] See Stardust Mission on the Homepage of the Jet Propulsion Lab at California Institute of Technology.

[28] Earth's galaxy consists of approximately 100 billion stars, and twenty galaxies comprise our cosmic neighborhood. Our solar system is only one humble unit in a supercluster 75 million light years in diameter. Moreover, since 1929, disciples of the man for whom the Hubble telescope is named have been demonstrating that the universe is expanding, and at an accelerating speed.

[29] Teilhard de Chardin, *Christianity and Evolution,* trans. Rene Hague (New York: Harcourt Brace Jovanovich, 1971) 241.

[30] In this the Victorian poet seems to anticipate the rejection by some twenty-first-century writers of the traditional Catholic teaching on redemption as the primary purpose of the Incarnation. See, for example, Michael Morwood, *Tomorrow's Catholic: Understanding God and Jesus in a New Millennium* (Mystic, CT: Twenty-Third Publishers, 1997) 31–35.

[31] Alice Meynell, "Christ in the Universe," in *The Poems of Alice Meynell* (London: Oxford University Press, 1940).

[32] Michael Morwood, lecture on "The New Cosmology," Stella Maris Retreat Center, Elberon, NJ, 14 March 2003.

[33] John 4:1-15.

[34] First proposed in the 1930s, the existence of dark matter and energy was confirmed by recordings at Wilkinson Microwave Anisotropy Probe, verified by Hubble, and officially recognized by The American Astronomical Society in 1993.

[35] Brian Greene, *The Elegant Universe: Superstrings, Hidden Dimensions, and the Quest for the Ultimate Theory* (New York: W. W. Norton, 1999) 225, 235.

[36] K. C. Cole, *The Hole in the Universe: How Scientists Peered over the Edge of Emptiness and Found Everything* (New York: Harcourt, 2001) 151.

[37] Lawrence Kraus, cited in Cole, *The Hole in the Universe*, 131.

[38] Lao-tzu, *Tao Te Ching: A New English Version by Stephen Mitchell* (New York: Harper and Row, 1988) Tao 1.

[39] Goldstein, *Psalms for the Cosmos.*

[40] Marcello Gleiser, *The Dancing Universe: From Creation Myths to the Big Bang* (New York: Dutton Penguin, 1997) 294.

[41] Although the phenomenon of black holes had been observed by astronomers for centuries, the term was coined as recently as 1969, when modern technology made it possible to describe how they were formed.

[42] Diarmuid O'Murchu, *Quantum Theology: Spiritual Implications of the New Physics* (New York: Crossroad, 2003) 12.

[43] Ibid., 185.

[44] Inspired by Dennis Overbye, "Life or Death: How Supernovas Happen," *New York Times* (9 November 2004) F1.

AFTERWORD

Writing a book, like every ordeal by fire, becomes a test of faith. Writing this one turned out to test my faith in faith itself. I undertook this project, not because I knew so much about science and spirituality that I wanted to tell, but because I had so many questions about the relationship between the two that I needed to ask. As the book progressed, I felt very keenly the presence of many mature religious men and women who, in opening themselves to "the new cosmology," have suddenly or gradually felt their commitment to truth becoming overshadowed by a fearful question: "Does embracing a new 'model of God' demand relinquishing the deep personal relationship that has been the center of meaning and the motive for commitment throughout my lifetime?" In my judgment, this critical question should be a matter of pastoral concern for those who make a living promoting the "new theology." Feminist theologian Sallie McFague acknowledges as much when she combines caution with reassurance in her influential work *Models of God:*

> I believe not only that the personal model is one of the central contributions of the Western tradition, *the loss of which would signal a paradigm shift of such proportions as to end that religious tradition,* but that it is possible to understand the personal model in a way that is compatible with (although not demanded by) contemporary science.[1]

My prayer is that these reflections have helped some readers to maintain and deepen that relationship. As I conclude these pages and continue my search, I would like to renew the personal conviction with which it began and add a condition that revealed itself as I prayed my way through these pages: the more we know about science, the deeper, more mature, and responsible our relationship with God can become, provided our quest for truth be accompanied by acts of faith. Although the church has always defined faith as a supernatural *gift*, it has also taught us to make "acts of faith." The title of these prayers implies that the gift must be continually and freely "exercised" and can never be taken for granted. Among the acts of faith I recommend is the reading of old books in tandem with new books. Often you will find "new" ideas about God either stated or implied in works as old as the psalms, where you missed their deeper significance until now. Works by and about men and women whose lives were formed and nourished by the basics of Christian dogma bear witness to the fact that faith neither dilutes nor denies intellect. People like Thomas Merton, Dorothy Day, Karl Rahner, Henri Nouwen, and Flannery O'Connor have come to my rescue whenever faith in my own intellect was faltering. With these trusted friends, I have come to understand the act of faith, not as a formulaic prayer, but as an act of will.

Over fifty years ago, on the Feast of Christ the King, Teilhard de Chardin seemed to be asserting an act of faith for all who have followed his lead in the search for God through the evolving revelations of science:

> There is undoubtedly a most revealing correspondence between . . . the two confronting Omegas: that postulated by modern science, and that experienced by Christian mysticism. . . . The Omegas of experience and of faith are undoubtedly on the point of reacting on one another in human consciousness and finally being synthesized.[2]

Teilhard expressed faith in a future that sometimes seems farther away from us than it was from him. That is because Teilhard the scientist hopes for the world to enjoy a synthesis that Teilhard the mystic has already experienced. When and if our understanding of God continues to change and grow, the approach to science as sacred metaphor can contribute to that synthesis.

> Contrary to popular opinion, theology is not a static and monolithic discipline. While it may not be as limber as science, it remains a dynamic enterprise.[3]

Neither science, art, nor secular humanism can compensate for a lost faith in God. Yet if science does not deepen our theology, it will surely displace it. What we spiritual people need to fear is not depth but superficiality. As more than one spiritual writer has pointed out, the opposite of "paranoia" is "metanoia"; the only escape from fear is conversion.[4]

Therefore, throughout this project I have repeatedly asked myself three questions, which I recommend to the reader:

- How does this information or insight resonate with my own experience of God?
- What does it demand of me?
- How might *living* this insight relieve pain or injustice in our world?

Cumulative answers to those questions have convinced me that God is even closer to us and more involved in our world than traditional faith had once imagined. Closer in very different ways, however. While I cannot let go of my personal God, that God is no longer enough for me. To maintain a relationship with my personal God, I must embrace a transpersonal God, by being more intimately involved with the world than I have wanted to be. "To be a *person*," writes Sallie McFague, "is to be the most sophisticated, complex, and unified *part of an organic whole that embraces all that is.*"[5] In freely responding, as a person to a Person, to the One in whom everything that is "lives and moves and has its being" we fulfill, not an inflexible design, but a sacred destiny.

In January 2005, scientists, commemorating the fiftieth anniversary of Einstein's greatest contributions to modern science, launched a series of events celebrating "The Year of Einstein." By mid-year, American politics had co-opted Einstein's spotlight for what could be called "The Year of Darwin." As usual, the popular press generated more heat than light. As I took refuge from the clamor in the peace of Mozart's *Requiem*, one of Einstein's favorites, I decided to conclude this volume by wondering what Einstein himself was thinking of it all.

Einstein Celebrates
(1955–2005)

"The mystery of conscious life perpetuates itself through
all eternity . . .
in the miraculous structure of the universe."

"Mozart's music is so pure and beautiful that I see it as a reflection
of the inner beauty of the universe."[6]

Albert Einstein

Safely free from space, time, thought
and quantum mechanics, Einstein now has
all the time in the world to listen.
What does he hear?

Beyond all ritual and requiem
background music assumes a foreground
as far beyond Mozart as
mystery beyond analysis.

Does one secret sound wave finally stir
this self-styled "deeply religious
non-believer" into certitude
beyond belief?

Beyond relativity, relationship.
Beyond unified theory, communion.
Beyond the last tremor of the superstring:
"music heard so deeply that it is not heard at all
but you are the music while the music lasts."[7]

Here at last
the whisper of the universe
is loud and clear enough
to wake the dead.

Elizabeth Michael Boyle, O.P.

NOTES

[1] Sallie McFague, *Models of God: Theology for an Ecological, Nuclear Age* (Philadelphia: Fortress Press, 1987) 97.

[2] Teilhard de Chardin, *Christianity and Evolution*, trans. Rene Hague (New York: Harcourt Brace Jovanovich, 1971) 243.

[3] Barbara Brown Taylor, *The Luminous Web: Essays on Science and Religion* (Cambridge: Cowley Publications, 2000) 19.

[4] Sam Keen, *The Passionate Life* (London: Gateway Books, 1983) 146.

[5] McFague, *Models of God*, 81.

[6] Quotations in the Einstein Exhibition at the American Museum of Natural History (New York: November 15, 2002–August 10, 2003).

[7] T. S. Eliot, "The Dry Salvages," in *The Complete Poems and Plays* (New York: Harcourt, Brace and Company, 1952).

GLOSSARY OF SCIENTIFIC TERMS

Besides serving as a quick reference for the precise meaning of terms, both familiar and unfamiliar, this glossary in itself can become a text for meditation. Private reflection on the scientific terms defined below, especially those used in the poems, will suggest additional metaphors related to personal and communal spirituality, to current history, and to Scripture. Definitions are adapted from the online science glossary at http://sci2.esa.int/glossary.

Absolute zero: The lowest temperature ever reached in this universe.

Adaptation: The adjustment of an organism to its environment; in microbiology, the adjustment of bacteria to a new environment.

Anthropic principle: The belief that everything in the universe is fine-tuned to generate human life and sustain it.

Antimatter: A particle with a different electric charge from a particle of matter. For every particle of matter that exists, there is a particle of antimatter.

Asteroid: One of billions of rocky objects less than 1000 km in diameter orbiting the sun.

Astrophysics: The study of the physical nature of all objects in space and the spaces between them.

Atom: Fundamental building block of matter, consisting of a nucleus and a swirl of electrons.

Big Bang: The theory which states that all the matter and energy of the universe originated in a tiny "point" that exploded 10 to 20 billion years ago and began the process of evolution. First proposed in the 1940s and confirmed in 1964 by the discovery of cosmic microwave background radiation.

Big Crunch: The theoretical point of gravitational pull at which the universe will implode.

Billion: One thousand million.

Black hole: An object with such a strong gravitational pull that nothing, not even light, can escape it; believed to be formed by the collapse of dying stars.

Comet: An icy body orbiting in space, characterized by two tails, one of gas and one of dust.

Cosmic background: Believed to be remnant radiation from the Big Bang.

Creationism: The belief that the origin of the universe is described accurately in the Book of Genesis.

Dark matter/energy: Matter or energy that cannot be detected by current instruments.

Darwinism/neo-Darwinism: The theory describing the process by which biological species evolved through millions of years of mutations adapted to the environment. Neo-Darwinism combines Darwin's theory of the "survival of the fittest" with contemporary genetics.

Dissipative structure: A new dynamic state of being resulting from a process of transformation out of chaos. (Term invented by Ilya Priogine, not included in online dictionaries.)

Earth: The third of the territorial planets counting 93 million miles from the sun.

Electron: A fundamental particle with a negative charge.

Entropy: Force directed toward disorder and decay.

Event horizon: The point after which there is no turning back.

Hubble Telescope (HUDF–Hubble Ultra Depth Field): An astronomer's instrument about the size of a school bus, launched into orbit April 25, 1990, from the cargo bay of a space shuttle. Every week it transmits data and images equivalent to a thirty-six-foot bookshelf.

Intelligent Design Theory (IDT): The argument that the complexity of matter requires the existence of design; "neo-creationism."

Light year: The distance traveled by light through space in one year. (ca. 5,880 billion miles).

Milky Way: A milky band of light comprised of ca. 100 million stars shaped like a disk with a circumference of ca. 100,000 light years.

Multiverse: The infinite number of universes that might exist beyond the one now known to science.

Nucleus: The central portion of an atom.

Neutrino: A fundamental particle with negative electric charge, possible source of *dark energy*.

Neutron: A particle without a charge, found in an atom.

Photon: A particle of light; the smallest unit of electromagnetic energy.

Planet: A large, spherical body of rock or ice orbiting the sun.

Proton: A positively charged constituent of the atomic nucleus.

Quanta: The smallest unit to which matter and energy can be reduced.

Quantum mechanics: Physics concerned with matter at the subatomic level.

Quark: An elemental particle believed to be the fundamental structural unit for all particles.

Quasar: A celestial object that resembles a star optically but is inferred to be an extremely remote and powerful source of light and radiation.

Relativity: Two theories by Einstein:
> *General relativity:* A geometric theory of gravitation which states that gravity causes space-time to curve.
> *Special relativity:* A theory which states that time is relative to the movement of the observer.

Star: A giant ball of gas with nuclear reactions at its core which produce vast amounts of energy.
> *Brown dwarf:* a failed star.
> *White dwarf:* a very dense star, no longer burning nuclear fuel.

String Theory: The theory that envisions the quantum universe as composed of tiny vibrating strings folded into particles, electrons, and quarks.

Symbiosis: A mutually beneficial relationship between two organisms.

Theory of Everything: The as yet undiscovered quantum-mechanical theory that embraces all matter and energy.

Time: The fourth dimension of reality.

Uncertainty principle: The theory attributed to Heisenberg that certain aspects of the microscopic world cannot be known with precision.

WORKS CITED

Allen, John C., Jr. "Catholic Experts Urge Caution in Evolution Debate." *National Catholic Reporter,* 29 July 2005, 5–7.

Baker, John Robert. "The Christological Symbol of God's Suffering." In Harry James Cargas and Bernard Lee, eds., *Religious Experience and Process Theology: The Pastoral Implications of a Major Modern Movement.* New York: Paulist Press, 1976, 93–103.

Baltazar, Eulalio F. *God within Process.* New York: Newman Press, 1970.

Balthasar, Hans Urs von. *Theo-Drama IV: The Action.* San Francisco: Ignatius Press, 1994.

———. *Theo-Drama V: The Last Act.* San Francisco: Ignatius Press, 1998.

Barbour, Ian. *Myths, Models, and Paradigms: A Comparative Study in Science and Religion.* New York and San Francisco: Harper and Row, 1974.

Barth, Karl. *Church Dogmatics: A Selection.* Trans. G. W. Bromley. New York: Harper Torchbooks, 1962.

Bavel, Torricius van. "The Creator and the Integrity of Creation in the Fathers of the Church." *Augustinian Studies* 21 (1990) 1–33.

Behe, Michael. *Darwin's Black Box: The Biochemical Challenge to Evolution.* New York: Simon and Schuster, 1996.

Blake, William. "Auguries of Innocence." *The William Blake Archive.* Ed. Morris Eaves et al. Washington, DC: Library of Congress. http://www.blakearchive.org.

Bohm, David. *Wholeness and the Implicate Order.* New York: Routledge and Kegan Paul, 1980.

Borckman, John. "What Do You Believe Is True Even Though You Cannot Prove It? The *Edge* Annual Question—2005." Edge: The World Question Center. http://www.edge.org.

Bruteau, Beatrice. "A Song That Goes On Singing: An Interview by Amy Adelstein and Ellen Daly." *What Is Enlightenment Online Magazine,* Spring/Summer, 2002.

———. *God's Ecstasy: The Creation of a Self-Creating World.* New York: Crossroad, 1997.

Bumiller, Elizabeth. "Bush Remarks Roil Debate on Teaching Evolution." *New York Times,* 3 August 2005.

Butkus, Russell. "Sustainability: An Eco-Theological Crisis." In Carol J. Dempsey, ed., *All Creation Is Groaning: An Interdisciplinary Vision for Life in a Sacred Universe.* Collegeville, MN: Liturgical Press, 1999, 144–167.

Chalmers, David. *The Conscious Mind: In Search of a Fundamental Theory.* New York: Oxford University Press, 1966.

Chang, Kenneth. "In Explaining Life's Complexity, Darwinists and Doubters Clash." *New York Times,* 22 August 2005, A1.

———. "Only in Quantum Physics: Spinning While Standing Still." *New York Times,* 9 September 2004, F3.

Clayton, Philip, and Arthur Peacocke, eds. *In Whom We Live and Move and Have Our Being: Panentheistic Reflections on God's Presence in a Scientific World.* Grand Rapids: Eerdmans, 2003.

Cole, K. C. *The Hole in the Universe: How Scientists Peered over the Edge of Emptiness and Found Everything.* New York: Harcourt, 2001.

Coston, Carol. *Permaculture: Finding Our Own Vines and Fig Trees.* San Antonio: Sor Juana Press, 2003.

Cousins, Ewert H., ed. *Process Theology: Basic Writings by Key Thinkers of a Major Modern Movement.* New York: Newman Press, 1971.

Dean, Cordelia. "Scientists Speak Up on Mix of God and Science." *New York Times,* 23 August 2005, A1.

Dembski, William. *Intelligent Design: The Bridge Between Science and Theology.* Downers Grove, IL: InterVarsity Press, 1999.

Dempsey, Carol J., O.P., ed. *Earth, Wind, and Fire: Biblical and Theological Perspectives on Creation.* Collegeville, MN: Liturgical Press, 2004.

———. "Hope amidst Crisis." In *All Creation Is Groaning.* Collegeville, MN: Liturgical Press, 1999.

Duve, Christian de. *Vital Dust.* New York: Basic Books, 1995.

Dobzhansky, Theodosius. "Teilhard de Chardin and the Orientation of Evolution." In *Process Theology: Basic Writings by Key Thinkers of a Major Modern Movement*. New York: Newman Press, 1971.

Eckhart, Meister. *Breakthrough: Meister Eckhart's Creation Spirituality in New Translation*. Trans. Matthew Fox. New York: Image Books, 1980.

———. *Meister Eckhart: The Essential Sermons, Commentaries, Treatises, and Defense*. Trans. Edmund Colledge and Bernard McGinn. New York: Paulist Press, 1981.

Edwards, Denis. "For Your Immortal Spirit Is in All Things." In Denis Edwards, ed., *Earth Revealing—Earth Healing: Ecology and Christian Theology*. Collegeville, MN: Liturgical Press, 2001, 45–61.

———. *The God of Evolution: A Trinitarian Theology*. New York: Paulist Press, 1999.

———. *Jesus in the Cosmos*. Mahwah, NJ: Paulist Press, 1991.

Eliade, Mircea. *Patterns in Comparative Religion*. New York: New American Library, 1958.

Eliot, T. S. *The Complete Poems and Plays*. New York: Harcourt, Brace and Company, 1952.

Ferguson, Marilyn. *The Aquarian Conspiracy*. New York: St. Martin's Press, 1980.

Fox, Matthew. *Meditations with Meister Eckhart: A Centering Book*. Santa Fe: Bear and Co., 1983.

Freitheim, T. E. *The Suffering of God: An Old Testament Perspective*. Philadelphia: Fortress Press, 1984.

Gamwell, Lynn. *Exploring the Invisible: Art, Science, and the Spiritual*. Princeton: Princeton University Press, 2002.

Gleiser, Marcello. *The Dancing Universe: From Creation Myths to the Big Bang*. New York: Dutton Penguin, 1997.

Goetz, Ronald. "The Rise of a New Orthodoxy." *Christian Century* 103, no. 13, 16 April 1986, 385–389.

Goldscheider, Erin. "Witches, Druids, and Other Pagans Make Merry Again." *New York Times,* 28 May 2005, B7.

Goldstein, Marion. *Blue Prints*. New School Chapbook Series. New York: New School University Press, 1999.

———. *Psalms for the Cosmos*. Johnstown, OH: Pudding House Press, 2003.

Gould, Stephen Jay. *Rocks of Ages: Science and Religion in the Fullness of Life*. New York: Ballantine Books, 1999.

———. *The Structure of Evolutionary Theory*. Cambridge: Belknap Press of Harvard University Press, 2002.

Grant, Edward. *The Foundations of Modern Science in the Middle Ages*. Cambridge: Cambridge University Press, 1996.

Greene, Brian. *The Elegant Universe: Superstrings, Hidden Dimensions, and the Quest for the Ultimate Theory*. New York: W. W. Norton and Company, 1999.

———. *Elegant Universe*. Written and directed by Julia Cort and Joseph McMaster. Based on *The Elegant Universe* by Brian Greene. Nova Productions, 2003.

———. *The Fabric of the Cosmos: Space, Time, and the Texture of Reality*. New York: Alfred Knopf, 2004.

Griffen, David Ray. *Archetypal Process: Self & Divine in Whitehead, Jung, and Hillman*. Evanston, IL: Northwestern University Press, 1990.

———. "Holy Spirit, Compassion, and Reverence for Being." In Henry James Cargas and Bernard Lee, eds., *Religious Experience and Process Theology: The Pastoral Implications of a Major Modern Movement*. New York: Paulist Press, 1976, 107–120.

———. *Process Christology*. Philadelphia: Westminster Press, 1973.

———. *Reenchantment without Supernaturalism: A Process Philosophy of Religion*. Ithaca, NY: Cornell University Press, 2001.

Griffiths, Bede. *A New Vision of Reality*. Springfield, IL: Templegate Publishers, 1983.

Hallman, Joseph M. "Toward a Process Theology of the Church." In Harry James Cargas and Bernard Lee, eds., *Religious Experience and Process Theology: The Pastoral Implications of a Major Modern Movement*. New York: Paulist Press, 1976, 137–145.

Hartshorne, Charles. *Omnipotence and Other Theological Mistakes*. Albany: State University of New York Press, 1984.

———. "Whitehead's Idea of God." In *Whitehead's Philosophy*. Lincoln: University of Nebraska Press, 1972.

Haught, John. *Deeper than Darwin: The Prospect for Religion in the Age of Evolution*. Boulder, CO: Westview Press, 2003.

————. *God after Darwin: A Theology of Evolution*. Boulder, CO: Westview Press, 2000.

————. *Mystery and Promise: A Theology of Revelation*. Collegeville, MN: Liturgical Press, 1993.

————. "Revelation." *The New Dictionary of Theology*. Ed. Joseph A. Komonchak, Mary Collins, Dermot A. Lane. Collegeville, MN: Liturgical Press, 1987.

————. *Science and Religion in Search of Cosmic Purposes*. Washington, DC: Georgetown University Press, 2000.

Haughton, Rosemary. *The Passionate God*. New York: Paulist Press, 1981.

Hellwig, Monika. *Jesus: the Compassion of God*. Wilmington: Michael Glazier, 1983.

Heschel, Rabbi Abraham. *Man's Quest for God: Studies in Prayer and Symbolism*. New York: Charles Scribner's Sons, 1954.

————. *The Prophets: An Introduction*. New York: Harper Colophon Books, 1955.

Hildegard of Bingen. *Hildegard of Bingen's Book of Divine Works with Letters and Songs*. Ed. Matthew Fox. Santa Fe: Bear and Co., 1987.

Hilkert, Mary Catherine, O.P., *Imago Dei: Does the Symbol Have a Future?* Santa Clara Lecture, vol. 8, no. 3. Santa Clara University, 14 April 2002.

Hirshfield, Jane. *Given Sugar, Given Salt*. New York: HarperCollins, 2001.

————. *The Lives of the Heart*. New York: HarperPerennial, 1997.

————. *Nine Gates: Entering the Mind of Poetry*. New York: HarperPerennial, 1998.

————. *The October Palace*. New York: HarperCollins, 1994.

————, ed. *Women in Praise of the Sacred: 43 Centuries of Spiritual Poetry by Women*. New York: HarperCollins, 1994.

Hodgson, Peter. *Winds of the Spirit: A Constructive Christian Theology*. Minneapolis: Fortress Press, 1994.

Hopkins, Gerard Manley. *Poems and Prose of Gerard Manley Hopkins*. Melbourne and Baltimore: Penguin Books, 1953.

Impastato, David, ed. *Upholding Mystery: An Anthology of Christian Poetry*. New York: Oxford University Press, 1997.

Isherwood, Charles. "Stories That Tell vs Storytelling." *New York Times,* 5 May 2005, E1.

Jantzen, G. *God's World, God's Body.* London: Darton, Longman and Todd, 1984.

John Paul II. "The Ecological Crisis: A Common Responsibility." Message on World Day of Peace, 1 January 1990. http://www.ncrlc.com/ecological_crisis.html.

———. "Lord and Giver of Life." Washington, DC: United States Catholic Conference, 1986.

———. "Message to the Pontifical Academy of Sciences on Evolution," 22 October 1996. *Origins,* 14 November 1996.

———. "Mulieris Dignitatem: Apostolic Letter on the Dignity and Vocation of Women." *Origins,* vol. 18, no. 17 (6 October 1998).

Johnson, Elizabeth A., C.S.J. *She Who Is: The Mystery of God in Feminist Theological Discourse.* New York: Crossroad, 1993.

———. *Truly Our Sister.* New York: Continuum, 2003.

———. *Women, Earth, and Creator Spirit.* New York: Paulist Press, 1993.

Johnson, George. "A Really Long History of Time." Rev. In *The Road to Reality: A Complete Guide to the Laws of the Universe.* New York: Alfred A. Knopf, 2005. *New York Times Book Review,* 27 February 2005, 14.

Jonas, Hans. *Mortality and Morality.* Evanston, IL: Northwestern University Press, 1996.

Kaufman, Gordon. *In the Beginning, Creativity.* Minneapolis: Fortress Press, 2004.

Keen, Sam. *The Passionate Life.* London: Gateway Books, 1983.

King, Ursula. *The Life and Vision of Teilhard de Chardin.* Maryknoll, NY: Orbis Books, 1996.

Knocke, Melanie Melton. *From Blue Moons to Black Holes: A Basic Guide to Astronomy, Outer Space, and Space Exploration.* Amherst, NY: Prometheus Books, 2005.

Koestler, Arthur. *The Act of Creation.* New York: Penguin Books, 1990.

Krugman, Paul. "Design for Confusion." *New York Times,* 5 August 2005.

Kuhn, Thomas. *The Structure of Scientific Revolutions.* Chicago: Chicago University Press, 1970.

Kunitz, Stanley. *Collected Poems.* New York: W. W. Norton, 2001.

———. *The Wild Braid: A Poet Reflects on a Century in the Garden.* New York: W. W. Norton, 2005.

Lane, Belden C. *Landscapes of the Sacred: Geography and Narrative in American Spirituality.* Mahwah, NJ: Paulist Press, 1988.

Lao-tzu. *Tao Te Ching: A New English Version by Stephen Mitchell.* New York: Harper and Row, 1988.

Lee, Bernard. "The Lord's Supper." In Harry James Cargas and Bernard Lee, eds., *Religious Experience and Process Theology: The Pastoral Implications of a Major Modern Movement.* New York: Paulist Press, 1976, 283–297.

Leone, Bruno J., ed. *Creationism vs. Evolution.* San Diego: Greenhaven Press, 2002.

Levertov, Denise. *The Great Unknowing: Last Poems.* New York: New Directions, 1999.

———. *The Life Around Us: Selected Poems on Nature.* New York: New Directions, 1997.

Lightman, Alan. *A Sense of the Mysterious: Science and the Human Spirit.* New York: Pantheon Books, 2005.

Lindberg, David C., ed. *God and Nature: Historical Essays on the Encounter Between Christianity and Science.* Berkeley: University of California Press, 1986.

Loewes, Anthony. "Up Close and Personal: In the End, Matter Matters." In *Earth Revealing—Earth Healing: Ecology and Christian Theology.* Collegeville, MN: Liturgical Press, 2001.

MacLeish, Archibald. *J. B.: A Play in Verse.* New York: Houghton Mifflin, 1986.

Margulis, Lynn. *The Symbiotic Planet: A New Look at Evolution.* New York: Basic Books, 1996.

———, and Dorian Sagan. *What Is Life?* London: Weidenfeld and Nielsen, 1995.

McFague, Sallie. *The Body of God: An Ecological Theology.* Philadelphia: Fortress Press, 1993.

———. *Models of God: Theology for an Ecological, Nuclear Age.* Philadelphia: Fortress Press, 1987.

McGrath, Alister. *Dawkins' God: Genes, Memes, and the Meaning of Life*. Oxford: Blackwell, 2005.

Meland, Benard. *The Realities of Faith*. New York: Oxford University Press, 1962.

Meynell, Alice. *The Poems of Alice Meynell*. London: Oxford University Press, 1940.

Miller, Kenneth R. "Darwin, Design, and the Catholic Faith." http://www.millerandlevine.com/km/evol.

Milosz, Czeslaw. *Second Space: New Poems*. New York: HarperCollins, 2004.

Moltmann, Jürgen. *The Crucified God: Science and Wisdom*. Trans. A. Wilson and John Borden. Minneapolis: Fortress Press, 1974.

———. *God in Creation: A New Theology of Creation and the Spirit of God*. Trans. Margaret Kohl. New York: Harper and Row, 1985.

———. *History and the Trinitarian God*. London: SCM, 1981.

———. *The Spirit of Life: A Universal Affirmation*. Minneapolis: Fortress Press, 1992.

Morwood, Michael. *Tomorrow's Catholic: Understanding God and Jesus in a New Millennium*. Mystic, CT: Twenty-Third Publishers, 1997.

Murphy, Nancey, and George F. R. Ellis. *On the Moral Nature of the Universe: Theology, Cosmology, and Ethics*. Minneapolis: Fortress Press, 1996.

Nesbett, Richard E., ed. *Human Inference: Strategies and Shortcomings of Social Judgment*. Englewood Cliffs, NJ: Prentice-Hall, 1980.

Nicholl, David. *Holiness*. Mahwah, NJ: Paulist Press, 1987.

Oliver, Mary. *American Primitive*. Boston: Back Bay Books, 1983.

———. *New and Selected Poems*. Boston: Beacon Press, 1992.

———. *Winter Hours: Prose, Prose Poems and Poems*. Boston: Mariner Books, 2004.

O'Murchu, Diarmuid. *Evolutionary Faith: Rediscovering God in Our Great Story*. Maryknoll, NY: Orbis Books, 2003.

———. *Quantum Theology: Spiritual Implications of the New Physics*. New York: Crossroad, 2003.

Overbye, Dennis. "Cosmos Sits for Early Portrait, Gives Up Secrets." *New York Times*, 12 February 2003, A1.

———. "Hunting for Life in Specks of Cosmic Dust." *New York Times,* 19 July 2005, F1.

———. "Images Reveal Deepest Glance into the Universe." *New York Times,* 10 March 2004, A1.

———. "Life or Death Question: How Supernovas Happen." *New York Times,* 11 September 2004, F1.

———. "Music of the Heavens Turns Out to Sound a Lot Like B Flat." *New York Times,* 16 September 2003, F3.

———. "A New View of the Universe." *New York Times,* 13 January 2004, F3.

———. "Quantum Theory Tugged, and All of Physics Unraveled." *New York Times on The Web.* http://www.nytimes.com/2000/12/12/science/12QUAN.html.

———. "Songs of the Galaxies, and What They Mean." *New York Times,* 3 August 2004, F1.

Palin, David. *God and the Process of Reality.* London: Routledge, 1989.

Pardington, G. Palmer III. "The Holy Ghost Is Dead—The Holy Spirit Lives." In Harry James Cargas and Bernard Lee, eds., *Religious Experience and Process Theology: The Pastoral Implications of a Major Modern Movement.* New York: Paulist Press, 1976, 121–132.

Plante, Judith, ed. *Healing the Wounds: The Promise of Ecofeminism.* Philadelphia: Fortress Press, 1984.

Polkinghorne, John. *Belief in God in an Age of Science.* New Haven: Yale Nota Bene, 2003.

———. *Science and Creation.* London: SPCK, 1989.

Powell, Samuel. *Participating in God.* Minneapolis: Fortress Press, 2004.

Prigogine, Ilya. *Order Out of Chaos.* New York: Bantam Books, 1984.

Rahner, Karl. "Christology within an Evolutionary View of the World." *The Life of the Dead.* Theological Investigations 4: *More Recent Writings.* Trans. Kevin Smyth. Baltimore: Helicon Press, 1966.

———. "Easter: A Faith That Loves the Earth." *The Great Church Year.* New York: Crossroad, 1993.

———. *Foundations of Christian Faith.* Trans. William V. Dych. New York: Seabury Press, 1978.

———. "The Resurrection of the Body." Theological Investigations 2: *Man in the Church.* Trans. Karl H. Kruger. Baltimore: Helicon Press, 1963.

Reagan, Michael, ed. *The Hand of God: Thoughts and Images Reflecting the Spirit of the Universe.* Philadelphia: Templeton Foundation Press, 1999.

Robinson, Marilyn. *Gilead.* New York: Farrar, Straus and Giroux, 2004.

Rockwell, John. "Move Over Middle C: The Speculative Case for the Cosmic B Flat." *New York Times,* 30 January 2004, E5.

Riley, Gregory. *The River of God: A New History of Christian Origins.* New York: HarperCollins, 2001.

Rilke, Rainer Maria. *Rilke's Book of Hours: Love Poems to God.* Trans. Anita Barrows and Joanna Macy. New York: Riverhead Books, 1997.

Russell, Robert John. "Contemplation in the Vibrant Universe: The Natural Context of Christian Spirituality." In *Center for Theology and the Natural Sciences Bulletin,* Autumn 1991, 5–16.

Safire, William. "Neo-Creo." *New York Times Magazine,* 21 August 2005.

Schnakenberg, Gjertrud. *Supernatural Love: Poems 1976–1992.* New York: Farrar, Straus and Giroux, 2000.

Schönborn, Christoph. "Finding Design in Nature." *New York Times,* 7 July 2005, A23.

Schwartz, John. "Smithsonian to Screen Movie That Makes a Case Against Evolution." *New York Times,* 20 May 2005, E1.

Seidel, Frederick. *The Cosmos Poems.* New York: Farrar, Straus and Giroux, 2000.

Siebert, Charles. "The Genesis Project." *New York Times Magazine.* 26 September 2004, 53–56.

Sobrino, Jon, S.J. *Christology at the Crossroads: A Latin American Approach.* Trans. John Drury. Maryknoll, NY: Orbis Books, 1978.

Solle, Dorothee. *Suffering.* Philadelphia: Fortress Press, 1975.

Stevens, Wallace. *Wallace Stevens: Collected Poetry and Prose.* New York: The Library of America, 1996.

Stout, David. "Frist Urges Two Teachings on Life Origins." *New York Times,* 20 August 2005.

Swimme, Brian. "Comprehensive Compassion." Interview. *What Is Enlightenment Magazine.* Spring/Summer, 2001.

————. *The Hidden Heart of the Cosmos.* Maryknoll, NY: Orbis Books, 1996.

Taylor, Barbara Brown. *The Luminous Web: Essays on Science and Religion.* Cambridge: Cowley Publications, 2000.

Teilhard de Chardin, Pierre. *Building the Earth.* Trans. Noel Lindsay. South Bend: Dimension Books, 1965.

————. *Christianity and Evolution.* Trans. Rene Hague. New York: Harcourt Brace Jovanovich, 1971.

————. *The Divine Milieu: An Essay on the Interior Life.* New York: Harper and Brothers, 1960.

————. *Future of Man.* London: Collins, 1964.

————. *The Heart of Matter.* Trans. Ursula King. London: Collins, 1978.

————. *Letters from a Traveler.* London: Collins, 1962.

————. "My Universe." Reprinted in *Process Theology: Basic Writings by Key Thinkers of a Major Modern Movement.* Ed. Ewert H. Cousins. New York: Newman Press, 1971.

————. *Phenomenon of Man.* Trans. Bernard Hall. New York: Harper Torchbooks, 1959.

————. *Toward the Future.* Trans. Rene Hague. New York: Harcourt Brace Jovanovich, 1975.

————. *Writings in Time of War.* London: Collins, 1968.

Toibin, Colm. "A Road Runs Through Tara." *New York Times,* 26 April 2005, A21.

Weinandy, Thomas G. *Does God Suffer?* South Bend: University of Notre Dame Press, 2000.

Wiesel, Elie. *Night.* London: SCM, 1981.

Wessels, Cletus. *Jesus in the New Universe Story.* Maryknoll, NY: Orbis Books, 2003.

Whitehead, Alfred North. *Process and Reality: An Essay in Cosmology.* New York: Macmillan, 1960.

————. *Symbolism: Its Meaning and Effect.* New York: Capricorn Books, 1959.

Wilford, John Noble. "Discovery of a First: A World with Three Suns." *New York Times,* 15 July 2005, A1.

Wilgoren, Jodi. "In Kansas, Darwinism Goes On Trial Once More." *New York Times,* 5 May 2005, A18.

———. "Politcized Scholars Put Evolution on the Defensive." *New York Times,* 8 August 2005, A1.

Zohar, Dana. *The Quantum Self: Human Nature and Consciousness Defined by the New Physics.* New York: William Morrow, 1990.

ACKNOWLEDGMENTS

The author gratefully acknowledges a profound and continuing debt to her science teachers, Sister Carmel Leifer and Sister Walter Proudfoot who inspired her earliest poetry, to poets Marion Goldstein and Mary McGuinness, O.P. for generous permission to reprint their work, to theologians Carol J. Dempsey, O.P. and Honora Werner, O.P., for their candid and constructive criticism, to John Schneider for his meticulous copyediting and to Mary Joseph Bircsak, O.P. for her scrupulous proofreading; above all, to those readers whose response to her first book gave her the courage to write another.

Permissions

"The Kingdom," from THE OCTOBER PALACE by Jane Hirshfield. Copyright © 1994 by Jane Hirshfield. Reprinted by permission of HarperCollins Publishers, Inc.

"Rock" from GIVEN SUGAR, GIVEN SALT by Jane Hirshfield. Copyright © 2001 by Jane Hirshfield. Reprinted by permission of HarperCollins Publishers, Inc.

"Da neigt sich die Stunde . . . / The hour is striking . . . ," "Wie durfen dich nicht . . . / We must not portray . . ." "Das bist der Arme, . . . / You are the poor one, . . ." from RILKE'S BOOK OF HOURS: LOVE POEMS TO GOD by Rainer Maria Rilke, translated by Anita Barrows and Joanna Macy. Copyright © 1996 by Anita Barrows and Joanna Macy. Used by permission of Riverhead Books, an imprint of Penguin Group Inc.

INDEX OF POEMS AND POETS

Titles are listed only for entire poems. Where the poet is cited "en passim," the poem is named in the accompanying endnote.

INDEX OF SCRIPTURE CITATIONS